Treasure of the Caves

Iris Noble

Treasure of the Caves

The Story of the
Dead Sea Scrolls

The Macmillan Company
New York, New York

PICTURE CREDITS: All of the photographs in this book are reproduced by the kind permission of John M. Allegro, with the following exceptions: Harris and Ewing News Service, 19; Israel Office of Information, 36, 39, 41, 107, 182–183; Palestine Archaeological Museum, 160 (bottom); Picture Archive of the Jewish Theological Seminary, New York, Frank J. Darmstaedter, Curator, 38, 95; Rapho-Guillumette, 123 (top), 151.

Maps by Rafael Palacios

Title page:
Aerial view of the Qumran excavation, showing the Dead Sea in the background and Wady Qumran lower right

The Macmillan Company
866 Third Avenue, New York, New York 10022

Collier-Macmillan Canada Ltd., Toronto, Ontario

Library of Congress catalog card number: 69–11303

10 9 8 7 6 5 4 3 2 1

This book is respectfully dedicated to all the men and women who contributed their scholarly knowledge and archaeological skills to the unfolding of the story of the Scrolls and the Qumran settlement. The author would particularly like to thank those who gave her their time for personal interviews, for correspondence, or for criticism of this book while in preparation.

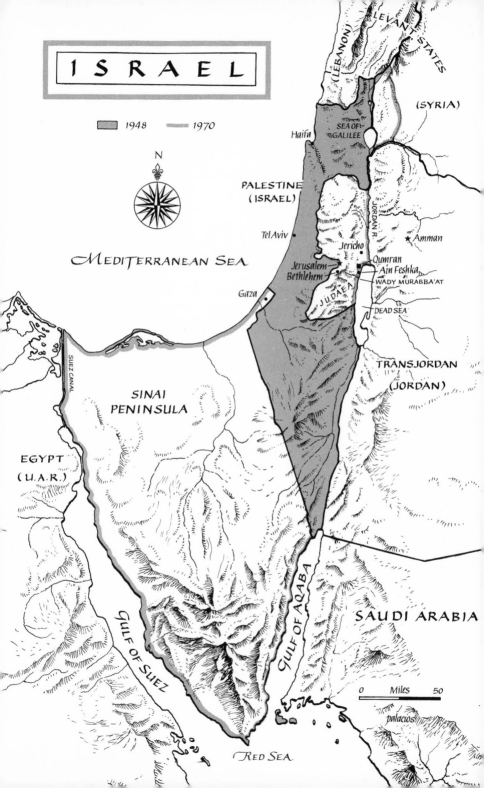

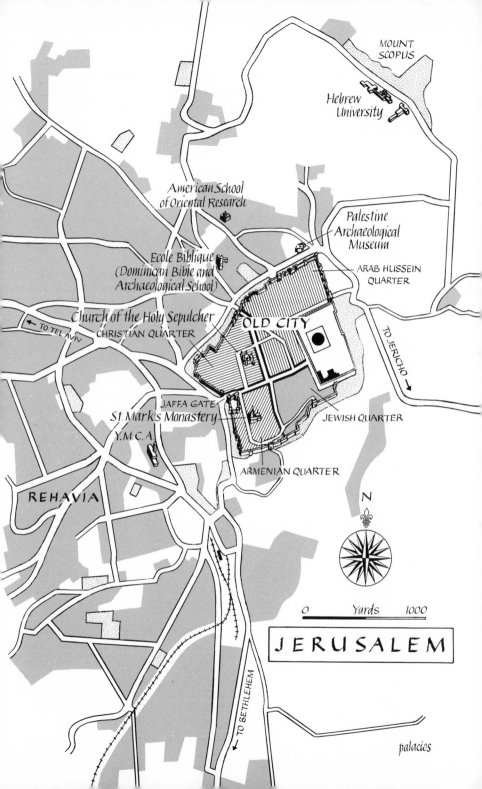

MOUNT SCOPUS

Hebrew University

American School of Oriental Research

Palestine Archaeological Museum

ARAB HUSSEIN QUARTER

Ecole Biblique (Dominican Bible and Archaeological School)

← TO TEL AVIV

Church of the Holy Sepulcher

CHRISTIAN QUARTER

OLD CITY

TO JERICHO →

JAFFA GATE

St. Mark's Monastery

Y.M.C.A.

JEWISH QUARTER

ARMENIAN QUARTER

REHAVIA

N

0   Yards   1000

JERUSALEM

TO BETHLEHEM

palacios

INTRODUCTION

IN THE MONTH OF JUNE, in A.D. 68, death came to Qumran in Judaea.

It was the time of the First Jewish Revolt. Judaea was part of one of the provinces of the Roman Empire, and in that year the Jews had risen in rebellion against their hated overlords, passionately determined not to accept foreign rule and foreign gods. In retaliation, the Roman general, Vespasian, led his legions through the country on a campaign of brutal punishment. Starting in the north he had traveled the length of the Jordan River valley southward, burning villages and slaughtering their inhabitants.

After putting the town of Jericho to fire and sword, he moved on a few miles south to the Dead Sea. Near the head of the sea, where the Jordan River emptied into it, was the road that crossed west over the mountains to Jerusalem. It was Vespasian's intent to move against that ancient city, but first he diverted his troops to destroy the Wilderness settlement, known today by the Arabic name of Qumran. There is no known record of what it was called two thousand years ago.

Possibly the Roman soldiers grumbled when they had to leave the main road and strike off across the stony, barren plain between the Dead Sea and the mountains, but Vespasian could not leave untouched even so remote and isolated a Jewish settlement as this. Although the community was a peaceful one, no men in Judaea were more stubborn in refusing to do homage to Roman dieties and in holding to their own God. They must be punished for this.

With the Dead Sea on their left, the legions marched diagonally across the plain. Their goal was one particular mountain of the Judaean ridge. It was formed something like a seated giant, with its great rocky breast and head joined to its neighbors, but with a lap of a high, sandy plateau that jutted out into the plain. The sides of the plateau fell down in silvery apron-folds, and on top of it stood the settlement of Qumran.

We can imagine the might and panoply of the Roman legions as they stormed the slopes and attacked the settlement. The Roman standards were carried to the front, the hot sun gleamed upon metal breastplates and shields, swords and battle-axes. The shouted orders echoed back from the mountainside, drowning out the prayers of the besieged. The defenders of Qumran fought bravely, but they were outnumbered and their homemade weapons splintered on the armor of the trained Roman soldiers.

They died valiantly, calling out the name of their God as they fell.

When the battle was over and the inhabitants lay dead, the Romans trampled the grounds and set fire to the settlement. Vespasian departed leaving only a few men behind to establish a police force.

Part of the compound on Qumran was rebuilt into a temporary military outpost. The soldiers were to patrol and keep a lookout for rebel fugitives, but there would not be much for them to do. Qumran was a desolate place, and the view from it was bleak. It is likely the soldiers were bored.

The area was known as the Wilderness, and the summer heat would have parched what little vegetation there grew on the rocky plain. The cool blue of the Dead Sea was an illusion: it was a salt lake, and only a few stunted plants grew along its infertile banks. Besides the soldiers on the plateau, the only inhabitants of this wasteland were rats, lizards, snakes, an occasional hyena and a few birds of prey.

Having little else to do, the Romans undoubtedly searched the ruins for loot. They must have been astonished when they found nothing. What manner of men were these plateau dwellers who had left no money, no jewels or other treasures?

There were hidden treasures here, but the Romans did not find them. Nor had they found them would they have considered them of any value, for the Qumran community's treasures were its holy scrolls. They were so sacred to the people of Qumran that even the letters, the ink and the leather they were written on were venerated. They were buried in secret "libraries," not only to protect them from destruction by enemies, but also to preserve them from rot and decay.

In A.D. 132–135 came the Second Jewish Revolt. This time the Romans struck back with devastating severity. Those Jews who were not killed were exiled by the thousands from Judaea. The Jewish population was reduced to a handful; people from surrounding areas moved in. Over the centuries Judaea became Arabian, and even its name was discarded. At the end of the First World War the British had a mandate over the area, divided between what was then Transjordan and Palestine.

In the spring of 1947 war was again a threat in Palestine. After the Second World War, mainly as a result of the terrible persecution of the Jews in Europe by the Nazis, Jews were returning to their ancient homeland in large numbers. They were met with resistance by both Arabs and the British. Nevertheless they came, yearning for their own nation once again. Circumventing the British prohibition to land, they arrived by shiploads in Palestine, where the Arabs saw them come with growing anger and mistrust.

Only in the Dead Sea wilderness, where no one now lived, where only nomads roamed, the angers of men still seemed far away. Here hawks circled in the lonely sky, rarely disturbed by the flight of an airplane, lizards flitted from rock to rock, and plateau and mountain guarded close the ancient secret of Qumran.

For two thousand years the hiding places of the sacred scrolls had remained undisturbed.

4

CHAPTER I

On a spring day in 1947 a boy named Muhammad
Adh-Dhib was searching for a lost goat.

The lad moved up the steep Judaean mountainside,
climbing swiftly as only a Bedouin can where there is no
path to follow. In places his sandaled feet slipped on the
limestone and loose shale. Occasionally he had to stop to
free his long robe when it caught on thorn bushes. He
was growing tired.

Although the sun was only mildly warm at this time of
year, he was hot from his scramble. He stopped just below
an overhanging crag. Beyond this the mountain steep-
ened, and even a goat could not have gone much farther.
Perhaps it would wander back of its own accord if Muhammad waited.

He sat down to rest beside a pinnacle of rock, leaning
his arms upon his knees.

From his high perch he could look eastward and downward upon the wide, rock, desert plain to the Dead Sea, across that lake to more wasteland and the far hills of Jordan. He could even catch a glimpse of sunlight on water to the north, where the river Jordan was bridged by the east-west road to Jerusalem.

Directly below him was a plateau where the rest of his flock of goats grazed. He had led them that morning to the plateau from the nearby oasis of Ain Feshka, where his tribe, the Ta'amireh Bedouins, were encamped. He watched the goats search for the tender green tufts that grew in springtime among the pebbles and marl and sand. Goats could live here but, as far as Muhammad knew, people could not and never had. His tribe was nomadic, roaming throughout the wilderness, visiting the town of Bethlehem only when it was necessary to sell or buy, carrying food and water with them since oases were scarce.

The plateau below him was Qumran.

He tilted his head back. The lost goat was still not in sight, but as the boy gazed around he noticed a hole in the rock face above him. This was not surprising. The mountainside was honeycombed with holes, cut by wind and water. Idly he picked up a pebble and tossed it into the dark opening.

Instantly he became alert. There had been a clinking sound which was not like rock striking rock. He threw another pebble and heard the same strange noise. He got to his feet, found a handhold and pulled himself up so that he could peer into the opening. For a second, because his eyes were used to the sun outside, he could see

6|

Entrance to Cave One: The upper opening is the one Muhammad first looked through. The lower one was made later by the Bedouins.

nothing but blackness. Then his eyes adjusted. Light filtered in behind his head. He was staring into a cave about twenty-five feet in length and six feet wide, high enough that a man could stand upright in it.

Muhammad had seen many caves in the mountains, but what struck him with wonder about this one were the contents—a number of great jars arranged in rows upon the ground. It was these his pebbles had struck.

They were of pinkish- and grayish-white clay. The smallest stood about twenty inches high, the tallest about twenty-seven inches, and the rest ranged between. The largest was bigger than any Muhammad had ever seen, and the shape was peculiar. Most were cylindrical, almost even in width from top to bottom. They stood upright on flat bottoms. The tops had a narrow clay ring at the neck, and over this a flat, bowl-shaped lid fitted tightly. One small jar had handles just below the lid. Some others were broken and lay scattered in jagged pieces. On the ground were also dark, torn pieces of something the boy could not identify.

Terrified, Muhammad loosened his hold and slid back. He rested in a crouching position on the ground. He was superstitious. He had never seen jars such as these, and he had been told that demons lived in caves. Had he disturbed the dwelling place of an evil spirit?

Just then the lost goat came into sight, slightly below him. Muhammad bounded down and chased the animal into a run. They slid and scampered as fast as they could until they reached the plateau. Even here the boy did not stop, but gathered up his flock and drove them down the high slope to the plain below. He wanted to get out of reach of the demons.

That night he listened to his elders speaking of the trouble brewing in Palestine between Arabs and Jews. They talked of war, but he thought of the cave. If he told them of the jars in the cave they might scold him for recklessness or for lying, but he had to confide in someone. So he whispered the story to a friend not much older than himself.

His friend was curious. The next morning found them both on the mountainside at the cave, their courage bolstered by each other's company. Perhaps it wasn't a demon's dwelling. Perhaps it was a robber's hiding place and his loot was inside those jars! The boys helped each other to climb inside the cave, where they opened the bowl-shaped lids.

They were disappointed. Many jars were entirely empty, and the rest held no jewels or money, only some objects that were leathery to the touch. They pulled out several of these objects and found them to be of different sizes and colors, ranging from cream to dark brown, but all of the same material, with bits of cloth sticking to it.

Whatever these objects were, they were in tight rolls, between two and six inches in diameter and from eight inches to a foot high.

The boys took a couple of the objects to the camp, where their elders were equally puzzled by them. The Bedouins did sometimes find strange things in the desert —ancient lamps or bowls or jewelry—but nothing like these. The older men went to the cave and brought out some jars and more rolls and carried them back to the camp. No one knows how many jars they took from the cave, or may have broken, or the number of scroll fragments that may have been lost through handling.

Upon close examination it was found that the objects were probably leather, because while some were brittle and hard, others were still soft and pliable to the touch. It would seem they once had cloth coverings, since rotten fragments of cloth still stuck to them here and there. One small roll was glued together by age; others could be loosened, and the largest, about six inches in diameter, though only ten and a half inches in height, could be unrolled without trouble.

To their amazement it stretched from one end of the tent to the other, and consisted of several sections sewn together. Even more astonishing was the fact that there was writing on the inside, most of it clearly visible although smudged in places. The Bedouins could not read it, but they thought the writing might mean that this object as well as the others might be worth some money.

At the time, the Bedouins attached little importance to their finds but were too cautious to throw them away. Under Palestinian laws all antiquities belonged to the government and were supposed to be handed over to the Department of Antiquities when found. Dealers in antiquities were required to register ancient objects and obtain permission from the authorities before selling them. But there were merchants in Bethlehem who bought old things without reporting such transactions. The Bedouins were poor, and part of their livelihood came from smuggling. They decided to take these strange finds with them when they went to Bethlehem to sell their cheese and some of their goat flock.

The Bedouins are vague, today, about how long they kept the jars and scrolls—in fact, some of them think the original discovery was made in November or December of 1946. By late March of 1947, however, they were in Bethlehem, where they showed two jars and some of the scrolls to an antiquities dealer named Feidi Salahi. At first Salahi would have nothing to do with them, because he thought the writing might be Hebrew and the scrolls stolen from a Jewish synagogue.

Much later, however, he did handle the sale of the jars and three of the scrolls.

The Bedouins were discouraged by Salahi's suspicions, but they happened to meet a man named George Shaya in the market place, to whom they showed the scrolls. At his suggestion they went to the shoe-repair shop of Khalil Iskander Shahin, a Syrian popularly known as Kando. Kando had several sidelines, and not all of a legal nature. After some haggling it was agreed that Kando and Shaya would try to sell the scrolls and give the Bedouins two-thirds of what they received. Kando was not given any of the jars.

The tribe returned to the desert, and with them, of course, went the boy Muhammad. He took no part in the transaction with Kando, nor in the talks with Salahi. After the discovery of the cave Muhammad, as befits a junior member of a tribal society, slipped back into obscurity.

After the Bedouins left, Kando and Shaya tried to make

out the writing on the leather scrolls. Both being Syrians, they hoped the language was ancient Syriac, because in that case they thought they knew of a buyer for them. Their own Archbishop, Athanasius Yeshue Samuel, presided over St. Mark's monastery in Jerusalem and was a learned man, proud of the valuable library of Syriac documents there. His title was Metropolitan, though he was often addressed as "Mar," a term of respect among Syrians.

Kando's and Shaya's interest in the scrolls had been lukewarm in the beginning. Kando had even told the Bedouins that at worst he might be able to use the leather for shoes. But now the thought of the Metropolitan as a possible buyer excited them. Shaya, who also had a business in Jerusalem making Bedouin cloaks, immediately left for that city to seek out Mar Athanasius.

At that time Jerusalem was a place of tension, of sporadic outbreaks of hostility between Jews and Arabs. The Arabs were alarmed at the rapid growth of the modern cities of Tel Aviv and Haifa, and at the talk of dividing Palestine into separate Arab and Jewish states. On the other hand the Jews were determined to have the security of their own nation once more, after two thousand years of exile and the terrible time of Nazi persecution.

While the United Nations debated the question of partition, the British remained in authority. The gates to the walled Old City were closely guarded and no one could

Kando's shop in Bethlehem

|13

enter without a pass. There was also a neutral zone, barricaded with barbed wire, and admission to this zone was almost as difficult. These measures were taken to keep the two enemy factions apart, but both Jew and Arab managed to slip through at times to plant a bomb.

The division of the city did not bring it peace. In daylight or in the darkness of night the sudden spatter of rifle fire could be heard. From rooftops snipers shot off a burst or two before they fled, and the bullets fell as often within the Old City as they did without.

Into this tension, on the Maundy Thursday of Easter week, 1947, Mar Athanasius led his monks from the monastery through the Old City streets to the Church of the Holy Sepulcher. It was an annual procession. The line of chanting monks moved through passageways so narrow that, in places, other people had to step back inside doorways to let them pass. The Metropolitan was preceded by a bodyguard of young acolytes, swinging censers. Their duty was to force a free space so the others could follow.

Carrying a gold crozier, the Metropolitan walked in solemn meditation, his long black and scarlet robes sweeping the old, worn stones of the streets. His heavy black beard gave him the appearance of a patriarch, although he was only middle-aged.

Shops lined the entire way. Buyers and sellers came and went, brushing by him or flattening themselves against walls to make way for the monks to pass. Hawkers cried their wares. Mar Athanasius had to make special efforts to concentrate upon his prayers on this holy day, but it was difficult to shut out the whispers of war he overheard in the street conversations. As Archbishop and Metropolitan he was responsible for the welfare of Syrians in the troubled lands of Jordan and Palestine, and his heart was heavy.

Suddenly he heard someone calling his name. He did not see the man until George Shaya appeared at his elbow.

"Your Grace, Your Grace!" Shaya called, breathlessly.

The Metropolitan halted. The procession stopped behind him. Mar Athanasius knew George Shaya as a member of his own congregation, and as a businessman. If Shaya interrupted a ceremony it must be for something important. But it was an improper thing to do.

"Can't it wait until I return to the monastery?" asked the Metropolitan.

"No, Your Grace," said George Shaya. What he had to say must be said immediately. Lowering his voice, he whispered that some very unusual scrolls with strange writing on them had been brought by Bedouins to a Bethlehem merchant. The writing might be Syriac. If St. Mark's monastery library was to acquire them, George Shaya must go immediately to Bethlehem or the merchant might sell them elsewhere. They had been found in a cave near the Dead Sea; they might be ancient.

The Metropolitan was a collector of rare manuscripts, and Shaya's excitement infected him. He wanted to see the scrolls. "Bring them on Saturday," he said.

At last the procession could continue, but the Metropolitan could not help thinking of what Shaya had told him. In ages past men had written their books on leather or papyrus in long strips which could be wound up compactly, and were called "scrolls." Nor were caves unlikely places to find such objects of antiquity. Just the same, the story Shaya had told him seemed almost too romantic to be true. The Metropolitan could only wonder and hope.

Shaya and Kando came to the monastery at the appointed time. The three men sat in Mar Athanasius' pleasant study, sipping thick, sweet, black coffee while they exchanged the formalities of Middle Eastern etiquette that precede all business transactions. Then Kando told the story in detail of how the Arab boy had found the cave and jars while hunting for a lost goat.

And inside those jars? With a dramatic gesture Kando unwrapped the newspaper package he had brought with him and showed the Metropolitan a brown object. Did the Metropolitan think this leather scroll was very old and worth anything? If so, Kando had others in his shop, and the Bedouins had still more. This one seemed in good condition, despite some cracks and broken edges.

The Metropolitan said nothing. He leaned forward and pressed a tiny section of torn edge between his thumb and forefinger. It crumbled into dust. Mar Athanasius nodded, satisfied; it was indeed old. New leather might be stained by exposure and appear aged but it would never turn into a powder when pinched. Just how ancient the scroll was, he could not yet say, nor could he, despite the powdering, yet be certain that it was leather.

He did something then that surprised the others. He asked George Shaya for a match, lit it, took another tiny fragment and burned it in the flame. Then he sniffed it.

Yes, he finally said, the test proved what the material of the scroll was. No matter how old or decomposed, leather when burned always gave off the same typical, scorched-flesh odor.

Then he unrolled one end and examined a section of the writing. It was in columns, much like that of a newspaper, with margins at top and bottom, and with regular spaces between the columns. Blank spaces indicated the end of a paragraph and the beginning of another. The

The Syrian monastery of St. Mark in the Old City of Jerusalem

columns were ruled in horizontal lines. The letters did not rest *on* the horizontal lines, but hung below with the tops of the letters just touching the lines.

The Metropolitan had a moment's sharp disappointment. The writing was not Syriac.

"Can Your Grace read this document?" Kando anxiously asked.

"No. It is written in Hebrew," said the Metropolitan.

Kando's face fell. A Christian Syrian monastery would have no interest, he was sure, in a Jewish scroll. He rose, bowing and apologizing, saying that perhaps George Shaya could find a Jew who would buy the rolls.

"Wait, my friend," Mar Athanasius interrupted him. "I wish to purchase them."

"But if they are not in your language, Your Grace," Kando asked in astonishment, "of what good will they be to you?"

"Do you want to buy all of them?" Shaya inquired.

Mar Athanasius ignored Kando's question but considered Shaya's. Could he be as sure of the rest, sight unseen, as he was of this one? He hesitated and asked when he could see them all. It was arranged that either Kando or the Bedouins would bring them to Jerusalem. No date was set. The Metropolitan watched Kando place the scroll back in its newspaper wrapping. Farewells were said and the two men departed.

Only then, when he was alone, could he allow himself to give way to the tremendous excitement he was feeling. His momentary disappointment that the scroll was not Syriac had been instantly replaced by a feeling that he had held in his hands a scroll so old it was beyond be-

Mar Athanasius Samuel

lief. Yet he did believe it. He had a strong hunch that the leather roll was two thousand years old.

Although he as yet had no proof, he has himself described the feeling of awe he experienced as he remembered the touch of the ancient leather and the strange story of the scroll's accidental discovery. A cave, sealed jars, ancient Hebrew letters—yes, it was possible. If so, was there any existing older document in the Christian-Jewish world than that scroll? He did not think so.

Words actually written when Jesus was alive!—and the Metropolitan knew a sharp anxiety that he had given this priceless manuscript back to Kando, who treated it with such carelessness that he had wrapped it in newspaper and would probably thrust it together with the others onto some crowded shelf in his shop.

For all his excitement, Mar Athanasius was cautious. The scrolls might be forgeries. Almost certain as he was of the one he had seen, he could not be sure of the rest. Kando and the Bedouins might have concocted the whole story. It was possible that this discovery of scrolls in jars in a cave had never taken place.

Genuine antiquities from the days of Roman occupation, or from the time of the Crusaders in medieval ages, had occasionally been found in Palestine and Jordan. They could be seen on exhibit in the Palestine Archaeological Museum or in the Hebrew University. But many Bethlehem or Jerusalem shops displayed "antique" articles that were really clever fakes. If lamps and vases could be forged, so could old writings, perhaps by employing an unscrupulous expert in old Hebrew, and by staining and smudging the leather.

The Metropolitan's mind warned him of such tricks, but his scholar's instinct was stronger. He wanted that scroll he had touched, and he wanted, intensely, to see the others. He waited, anxiously, to hear, but months went by without word from Kando. He might have found another buyer.

When the Metropolitan had almost given up hope, a message was delivered to him. The Bedouins, not Kando, would bring the scrolls to the monastery before noon on July 21.

All morning on that day Mar Athanasius waited, watching the clock. Every moment he expected one of his monks to knock on his study door to say that Bedouin strangers wished to see him. By twelve noon he knew it was too late. The appointment had not been kept.

When he joined the rest of his monks in the dining hall he scarcely listened to the talk around him. Suddenly his attention was caught. One monk was telling the others, with indignation, how ragged Bedouins had dared to bring some filthy manuscripts to the monastery gates, where they had insisted upon seeing Mar Athanasius. The monk had sent them away.

"You did what, Father?" The Metropolitan's spoon dropped to his plate. "I have been waiting for them all morning."

He quickly left the table to telephone Kando. But as he entered his study the phone was already ringing. Kando was much upset. The Bedouins, he said, had been insulted, and now they might take their scrolls to another merchant.

George Shaya finally persuaded the Bedouins to give the Metropolitan another chance. He had become friendly with the Ta'amireh, and they had twice taken him to see the cave. More scrolls were recovered from it, and the Bedouins had entrusted Kando with the sale of some of them. They gave the others to the merchant Salahi, who by this time had become convinced that the scrolls had not been stolen.

On August 5, Shaya and Kando accompanied the two Bedouins to St. Mark's monastery. They brought with them five scrolls, including the one the Metropolitan had already seen. After the usual coffee had been drunk, Mar Athanasius gently uncurled every scroll except one, which was so glued together by decomposition it could not be pulled open. He examined them briefly. The writing was faded in places but in others strikingly clear. Instinct had told him that the first scroll was genuine, and the other four seemed equally old.

The time had come to discuss the price. The Metropolitan had already decided he had no right to use St. Mark's money. Library funds were allotted for buying Syriac documents, not Hebrew scrolls. He would pay for the scrolls out of his own pocket, from his meager savings; then he alone would suffer should they prove to be forgeries.

It was customary in Jerusalem to bargain and haggle, but he thought it would be more effective to be frank with the Bedouins. He brought out his purse. "This is all the money I have in the world, my friends," he said. "I can offer no more than this." The pounds he put on the table were the equivalent of about two hundred and fifty dollars.

He had done the right thing, or perhaps it was more than Kando and the Bedouins expected. Their eyes lit up and Kando reached eagerly for the money. The Bedouins were smiling as they stood up to say good-by, and took their leave in good humor.

At last the Metropolitan was alone with the scrolls.

They lay on the table before him. He opened the end of one and stared at it. Stained and dirty, it was beautiful to him.

He was gambling on his hope that the scrolls were so ancient they would be worth a lot of money. He treasured them for their historic value, but they also represented a chance to help his people, if he could sell them. The Syrian Christian churches and their congregations were poor. Looking at the scrolls, the Metropolitan envisioned the possibilities of feeding and clothing the needy, repairing the monastery, and even building other splendid churches to the glory of his Christian faith.

He gathered up the scrolls and put them carefully on a library shelf. What was written on them was not his main concern. They might be the accounting of a rich man's estate. They might be anything. Mar Athanasius did not know.

First, the truth of the Bedouins' story must be tested. George Shaya and a monk from St. Mark's, Father Yusif, upon whose astute judgment the Metropolitan frequently depended, went with the Ta'amireh to the cave, and reported spending a night there in the stifling Dead Sea heat. Father Yusif described what he had seen to the Metropolitan: scraps of scrolls on the floor of the cave, but no complete one, and pieces of wood and broken pottery.

There was also one empty jar. Father Yusif had thought of taking it to a Syrian monastery not far north of the Dead Sea, where it might be used for storing cold water. He had rejected the idea because of the effort of carrying it so far on such a hot day and had left it in the cave.

The Metropolitan was now convinced that the story of the discovery in the cave was true. Of course, the evidence could have been planted there, but he did not think so. He was certain the scrolls had been found by accident, and was becoming more and more confident of their great age.

The first persons to whom he showed the scrolls tried to discourage such an idea.

Stephan Hanna Stephan, a member of the Palestinian Department of Antiquities, thought they were fakes. He would not even consider reporting them to Mr. R. W. Hamilton, Director of Antiquities, since he thought he'd be laughed at.

Father J. van der Ploeg, who was visiting Jerusalem and staying at the French Dominican Bible and Archaeological School (École Biblique), also examined them but could not credit the Metropolitan's feeling that they were very old, nor did he believe the Bedouins' story. If they had been found in jars in a cave, where was a jar to prove it? The Metropolitan could not produce one, and Father van der Ploeg remained skeptical.

But he was a scholar of paleography and could read the script of the largest scroll, which he positively identified as a book of Isaiah! The information excited the Metropolitan, especially when van der Ploeg told him that if this were really two thousand years old it would be worth a million dollars or more. A price could hardly be put on a Biblical scroll of that age. No, he cautioned the Metropolitan, this was probably a few centuries old, a valuable addition to the monastery library, but no more than that. It was always the custom of Jewish scribes to hand-copy new Biblical scrolls from old ones. The old ones were never destroyed but were stored in a place called a *genizah*. A cave was an unusual place for a *genizah*, but it might have served some medieval scribe or synagogue. As for the idea that these scrolls had been preserved since the time of Jesus because they were in jars—where were the jars? again asked van der Ploeg.

The next man to see the scrolls was Mr. Toviah Wechsler, of the Hebrew University. He also discounted their antiquity. "Your Grace," he said, indicating the scrolls and the table on which they lay, "if these came from the time of Christ as you imply, you couldn't begin to measure their value by filling a box the size of this table with pounds sterling."

In spite of these opinions Mar Athanasius maintained his stubborn belief in the great antiquity of the scrolls. The more convinced he became of their worth, the more cautiously he moved.

He could easily have picked up the telephone and called Mr. Hamilton at the Palestine Archaeological Museum and asked for an expert to study the scrolls. There were permanent "schools" in Jerusalem, financed and staffed by foreign scholars, such as the American School of Oriental Research. These organizations were responsible to the Palestinian Department of Antiquities. Mr. Hamilton, himself, had no expert knowledge of old languages and scripts, but he would have known of others, resident at these schools, who were paleographers.

Like the Bedouins, the Metropolitan feared the Department of Antiquities would want the scrolls, as they had the right to claim any recent discovery in Palestine. Mar Athanasius wanted to sell them, not have them confiscated. The question of the rightful ownership of the scrolls was to come up time and again in the ensuing years, but it was never a question with the Metropolitan. They were *his*.

He thought the most likely place to find an expert and a buyer for the scrolls would be at the Hebrew University. With the deepening hostility between Arabs and Jews it was no longer an easy matter for a Jew to come into the walled city to the monastery, and equally difficult for a Syrian to go into the Jewish quarters outside the walls. Secretly, the Metropolitan asked the help of a friend, Anton Kiraz. Could Kiraz find someone who was enough of a scholar to read an old Hebrew manuscript, wealthy enough to buy, and discreet enough not to talk about the transaction?

CHAPTER II

IN OCTOBER AND NOVEMBER of 1947 archaeologists in Jerusalem had something on their minds besides scientific matters. Palestine was on the brink of war, making ordinary pursuits difficult and even hazardous.

Dr. Elazar L. Sukenik, Professor of Archaeology at the Hebrew University in Jerusalem, returned that autumn from a trip to America, glad to be back with his wife and family, his books and his work, but particularly anxious to be in Jerusalem at this moment when the question of partition and the creation of a Jewish state was soon to be decided. The debates in the United Nations were coming to a close and soon the vote would be taken. There seemed no possibility that the Jews and Arabs could exist side by side in one nation, as neighbors, because of the passionate longing of the Jews for a place of their own, and the equally passionate hatred of the Arabs against a people they considered intruders.

All over Jerusalem men gathered in the doorways of shops to listen to the United Nations debates over the radio. In the streets of the city men walked nervously, restlessly, thinking of the possible terrors to come, waiting for the word that would bring joy or disappointment. Professor Sukenik hoped the decision would be for an Israeli state, but he knew the situation was explosive. If the vote went for partition the Arabs were certain to resist it with arms. One of the professor's sons was General Yigael Yadin, Chief of Operations of the Haganah, a Jewish liberation organization. In peacetime the son, like his father, was an archaeologist, but if war came he would be in the thick of the fighting.

On Sunday, November 23, Dr. Sukenik went as usual to his office at the Hebrew University on Mount Scopus. There he found an urgent message from an Armenian antiquities dealer he knew, asking that Dr. Sukenik get in touch with him. Over the telephone they agreed to meet the next day at the gateway of Military Zone B. This was one of the neutral zones where the British, who still held their Mandatory power over Palestine, had their headquarters. It was barricaded and guarded; only those with a pass could enter it.

From the Jewish quarter, Rehaviah, where his home was, Dr. Sukenik walked up the street the next morning and halted at the gate. He had no pass to enter, but from the other side of it he could see the dealer approaching. When they faced each other, with the wire gate between them, the Armenian held up a piece of leather. Dr. Sukenik could just make out some writing on it.

With his face close to the wire mesh, under the watchful eyes of the British guard, the dealer told a curious story. This fragment of leather was from some scrolls that Bedouins had brought to Salahi, the Arab antiquities dealer in Bethlehem, saying they had been found in a cave near the Dead Sea. In turn, Salahi had brought the fragment to the Armenian dealer, asking him to get in touch with Dr. Sukenik to find out if it was old and genuine.

Did Dr. Sukenik think the story could be true? Was he interested? Would he want to buy this fragment and the scrolls for the Hebrew University?

The professor leaned as close as he could get, trying to decipher the writing. It was certainly Hebrew, but not a modern or even a well-known Hebrew script. But as he moved his head to see the fragment more clearly, the letters suddenly became decipherable. Dr. Sukenik had recently been doing a special study of ossuaries, the limestone burial chests used by Jews in the period of around 40 B.C. to A.D. 70. The script on those ossuaries was the same as the script on this fragment! The script would date the scrolls as having been written in that same period.

He doubted the evidence of his own eyes. It could not be. He had never seen such script on leather. He had long been convinced, as other archaeologists were, that no scrolls of leather, parchment or papyrus could survive many centuries of the Palestinian climate.

Seeing his perplexity, the dealer told Dr. Sukenik he would bring more such fragments from Bethlehem to his own shop, where the professor could examine them closely.

On Thursday, November 27, the dealer telephoned to say he had more pieces. Dr. Sukenik had in the meantime arranged for a pass; armed with it he passed through the Zone B gate and made his way to the Armenian's shop. Here he was shown several fragments and could study them. There was no question in his mind, then, but that the script was the same as the carved Hebraic inscriptions on the limestone chests, a Hebrew script two thousand years old.

Dr. Sukenik was stunned. His reason told him that no manuscript scraps as old as these could still be in existence—but was it not possible, after all? The desert was dry in the Dead Sea area for almost all of the year. If the scrolls had been sealed inside wrappings, then placed in jars and stored in a cave, could they not have been thus miraculously preserved?

If he wanted to see all the scrolls, the dealer told him, he would have to go to Bethlehem. It might be dangerous. Bethlehem was populated almost entirely by Arabs. But Dr. Sukenik had the courage of a man dedicated to his profession. He agreed to go to Bethlehem, and arrangements were made.

His family begged him not to go. It was not safe. Tension on both sides was at trigger point, since the United Nations' decision was expected the next day. It had even been rash to enter Zone B despite his pass. His son, Yigael Yadin, as an archaeologist, sympathized with his father's yearning to see the scrolls, but he was also an army general and must advise against it. For a Jew to venture into Bethlehem at this time was a hazardous undertaking.

Dr. Sukenik knew his family was right. He was to go to Bethlehem the following morning, but postponed the appointment. That night, however, he listened to the radio and found the final vote on the "Jewish State" resolution had been put off another day by the United Nations. It seemed to him he must seize this opportunity. Once the vote was taken, war might come in earnest.

The next morning, November 29, he left the house early, used his pass again to go through the Zone B gate, and met the Armenian dealer. Their destination lay some five miles directly south of Jerusalem. They got on a bus, and the journey did not take long. Both men were frightened, but they arrived safely.

The dealer led the way through the narrow, twisted streets of the small town to the shop of Feidi Salahi. In his attic they sipped coffee while the Bethlehem dealer told them of how the Bedouins had come to him with some rolls of leather that they had found near the Dead Sea. A stray goat had led to the discovery of a cave and of eight earthenware jars in which the leather "bundles" were concealed.

Professor Sukenik listened intently. The story had an air of truth about it. Then the dealer brought out two jars for his inspection.

The archaeology professor was instantly aware that these jars were unique. Had they been faked, surely the forger would have made them look like the jars in common use around the first century. These were obviously different from any drawing or description of Palestinian pottery.

Dr. Sukenik was trembling now, with awe and hope. The dealer handed him one of the scrolls. The professor unrolled a part of it and began to read. The language and script were again similar to what he had taught himself to read from the limestone chests, and he found he could understand the words.

Scanning the columns his eyes picked out clear words and sentences here and there. They had the rhythm and beauty of the Psalms. They were, however, not the Bible Psalms but hymns much like them, hymns of thanksgiving to God.

Now he was absolutely convinced. The scrolls had to be genuine. Someone might have forged an ostensibly ancient manuscript of an Old Testament book but not a completely original work. This scroll was the work of an unknown Hebrew poet. Who could have written it? Why was it not a part of the ancient Jewish cultural traditions? For, judging from the script, he was certain it was at least two thousand years old.

The shrewd dealer was watching his face. Dr. Sukenik tried to appear composed. The time had come to buy, but he had no money with him.

Could he take the leathers home with him, to study them further? There were four bundles of them, and at that time Dr. Sukenik spoke of "leathers" since he could not be sure how many scrolls there were, and whether the fragments made up complete scrolls, or were parts of other manuscripts.

The dealer agreed. If Dr. Sukenik wished to buy them, after examination, the purchase price would be fifteen hundred English pounds, or about forty-two hundred American dollars.

Dr. Sukenik did not know that other scrolls had already been sold to the Metropolitan, for only two hundred and fifty dollars. It is still not clear whether the two Bethlehem dealers were working independently of each other or not; whether the Bedouins had trusted Kando with part of their discovery and Feidi Salahi with the rest—or whether Kando was behind all the negotiations.

The scrolls were wrapped in paper and Dr. Sukenik walked out carrying them under his arm. As he and his friend waited for the bus he was aware of the unnatural atmosphere in the town. Business seemed at a standstill, and groups of Arabs gathered in the streets to talk of the approaching war.

What was he doing here—a middle-aged scholar and unarmed? At last the bus came. They rode back to Jerusalem. As he parted from his Armenian friend, the latter said: *"Al-hamdulillahi*—thank God we have returned safely!"

As soon as he arrived home Dr. Sukenik shut himself in his library and spread out the leathers. One scroll he put aside; it was so stuck together it would take time and an expert to unroll it. Another scroll was made up of three sheets of leather sewn together. He could not be certain of the other bundles until all the large and small pieces had been studied.

He glanced at the writing, here and there, but the texts

were strange to him. Two days later he was able to put through a telephone call to inform the Armenian dealer that the sale was definite. Dr. Sukenik knew he had found a cultural treasure in the scrolls, and was willing, if necessary, to mortgage his house to buy them for the university.

On that same evening, the twenty-ninth of November, he was once more in his library poring over the fragments. He could not leave them alone, even though the whole city of Jerusalem was in ferment. The United Nations' decision was expected within hours.

In the next room his younger son was listening to the radio. Suddenly he rushed into the study. The vote had carried in favor of partitioning Palestine and making one part of it a Jewish state! At last the Jews had their homeland; its name was to be *Israel*.

Along with everyone else Professor Sukenik rushed out into the streets, where the joyful crowds were singing and dancing, weeping and shouting with happiness. He was caught up in the festivities, but not even then could he forget the scrolls. He saw friends and tried to tell them how fitting it was that on this night another part of their ancient heritage had been returned to them, but it is doubtful they understood, so great was the noise.

Tears of joy and thankfulness were in Dr. Sukenik's eyes. The celebration that night was all the more emotional for what tomorrow might bring.

Indeed, the morning brought what was expected. The Arabs denounced the United Nations' decision and declared they would not abide by it. Attacks and retaliations, on both sides, grew more frequent; a bus or taxi ride was a hazardous journey; between Jewish and Arab quarters there were intermittent bursts of rifle or mortar fire. Only the presence of British troops, who would not leave the area until their mandate was ended the following spring, kept some measure of communication open between all sections of Jerusalem, and held back the outbreak of total war.

The normal course of work was difficult, but it went on. Dr. Sukenik told the Hebrew University librarian of his purchase. To his astonishment, Dr. Sukenik now learned that the librarian knew of the existence of more of the scrolls, at the St. Mark's monastery, which the Syrian Metropolitan wanted to sell. From the story and description the professor was certain his scrolls and the Metropolitan's came from the same Bedouin source.

He got permission from Dr. J. Magnes, the University president, to handle the matter should the Metropolitan open negotiations to sell the scrolls in his possession.

Then he turned his attention to the scrolls he had. Dr. Sukenik's diary (he died in 1952) does not state the precise circumstances of payment for them, nor does it mention the purchase of the two jars he had seen in Bethlehem. It is only known that he did acquire those jars and the leather "bundles" at this time, for the Hebrew University.

He was most fortunate to find an expert in handling and unrolling the leather pieces, Dr. J. Biberkraut. Dr. Sukenik had been afraid to manipulate some of them for

|35

Dr. Biberkraut examining one of the ancient scrolls

fear of damaging them. Now he could begin the task of reading and studying the ancient script.

There were three scrolls, two of them in fragments of various sizes that had to be pieced together. Neither he nor Dr. Biberkraut attempted at this time to unroll the third one, which seemed to be intact, although later they were to find that several of the fragments belonged to it.

Of the first two, they called one the Thanksgiving Hymns. Dr. Sukenik had read a part of one of these hymns, similar to the Psalms, in the Bethlehem merchant's shop. The Thanksgiving scroll came in two rolls, and this fact had led Dr. Sukenik to believe at first he had four scrolls, not three. One part was large, consisting of three sections sewn together. The other part fell into seventy fragments when opened. Originally, both parts must have constituted one long scroll.

The second scroll came in five sections, damaged at the bottom, presumably from dampness, despite the protection of its container. Its contents seemed to be of a religious nature, but dealing with preparations for a war. Dr. Sukenik realized it would require considerable study to relate it to the Jewish religious-historical life of the period.

In both scrolls he noted a poetic and beautiful use of language. He worked slowly, always conscious he was handling manuscripts whose very existence was a miracle. The ancient Hebrew script was not difficult to read, but he had to accustom himself to the peculiar handwriting of each scribe, to words being broken by the separation of sections and fragments, and to gaps in sentences when words were obliterated by age. And always he thought, anxiously, of the other scrolls in St. Mark's monastery.

When the message came it was not through Dr. Magnes. In a strange way, it came directly to him. The ossuary chests that two years earlier Dr. Sukenik had studied had been found on property belonging to a Syrian named Anton Kiraz. This was the same Kiraz the Metropolitan had enlisted to help him, and now, near the end of January, 1948, came a letter from Anton Kiraz saying that he had some old scrolls to sell. The letter had taken three days to cross no more than a few streets.

A rendezvous was set in the Y.M.C.A. Although it was a favorite meeting place for Arab leaders, it was located

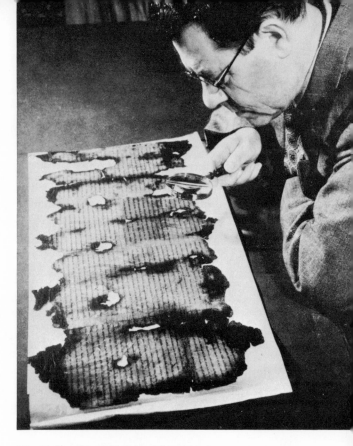

*Dr. Sukenik examining fragments
of the Thanksgiving Hymns*

in neutral Zone B, and Dr. Sukenik had no choice but to agree. Carrying books, he approached the building. Arabs lounged on the steps. Their long robes were the usual garb of Palestinians, but many city-dwelling merchants were beginning to adopt the European business suit, such as Dr. Sukenik wore. He could only hope to be taken for such a merchant, returning books borrowed from the Y.M.C.A. library.

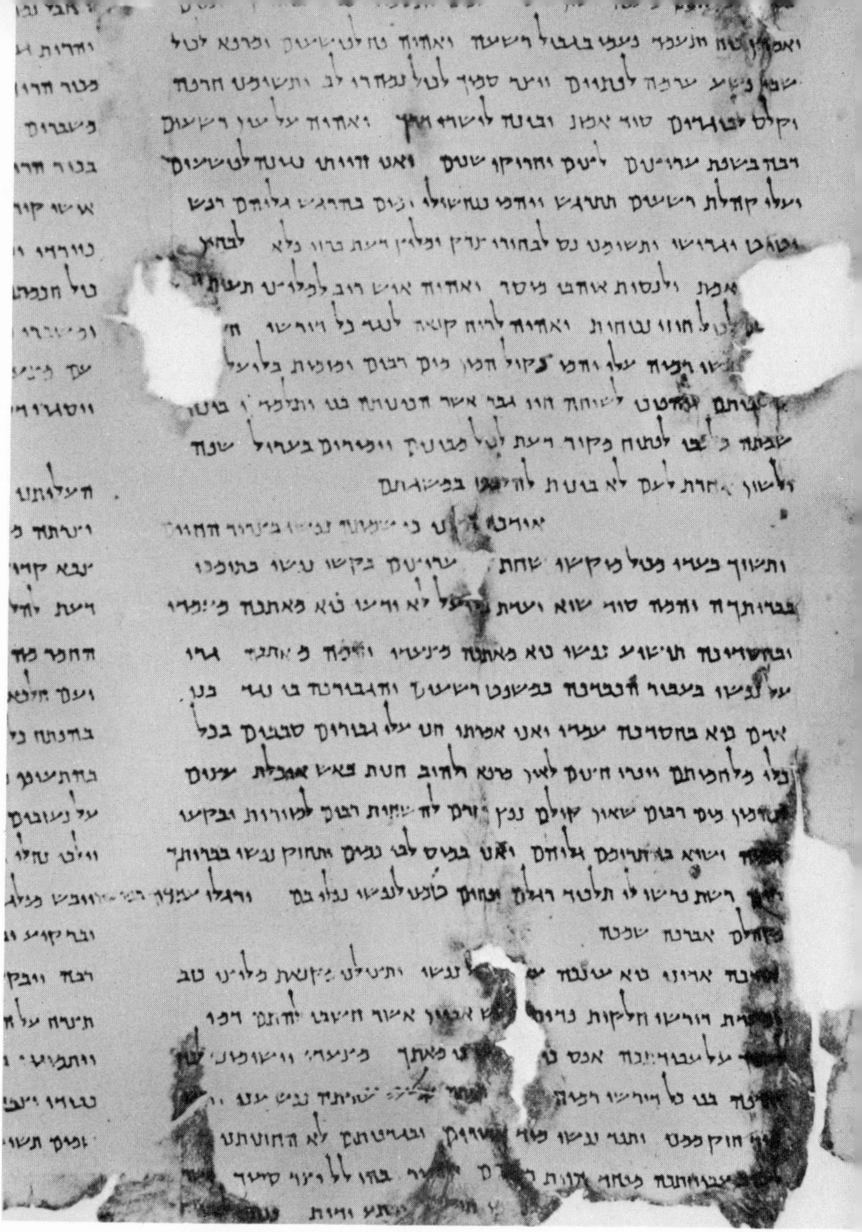

Detail of the Thanksgiving Hymns

Evidently he excited no suspicion. He was given only a casual scrutiny as he walked up the steps and into the building. There he found Anton Kiraz waiting for him in a private room. Three scrolls were brought from the Y.M.C.A. safe and placed on a table before Dr. Sukenik.

It needed only a glance to tell him these scrolls had the same look of great age as the ones he had bought from Salahi, even without the similarity of the story Kiraz told, of their discovery in a cave by Bedouins. These three seemed to be complete, intact scrolls, and he could easily unwind the end of the largest one and spread it out on the table. To his immense joy, he found it was the Old Testament book of Isaiah, and from the great length of the scroll, as he unwound it farther, he guessed it probably contained the entire book.

As he read, Kiraz talked. He said the Metropolitan had bought them from the Bedouins, but finding himself in straitened financial circumstances had accepted money from Kiraz, a prosperous businessman, and had made him his partner in the ownership of the scrolls. Therefore, Kiraz was empowered to negotiate a sale.

(In later years the Metropolitan denied the partnership, but Anton Kiraz stoutly maintained that it was a fact.)

Dr. Sukenik assured Kiraz that he would purchase the scrolls if he might first take them home and study them. Kiraz gave his permission, and the end of the week was set as the deadline. The scrolls must be returned to the Y.M.C.A. by then, with or without an offer.

Dr. Sukenik was positive the Jewish Agency which was

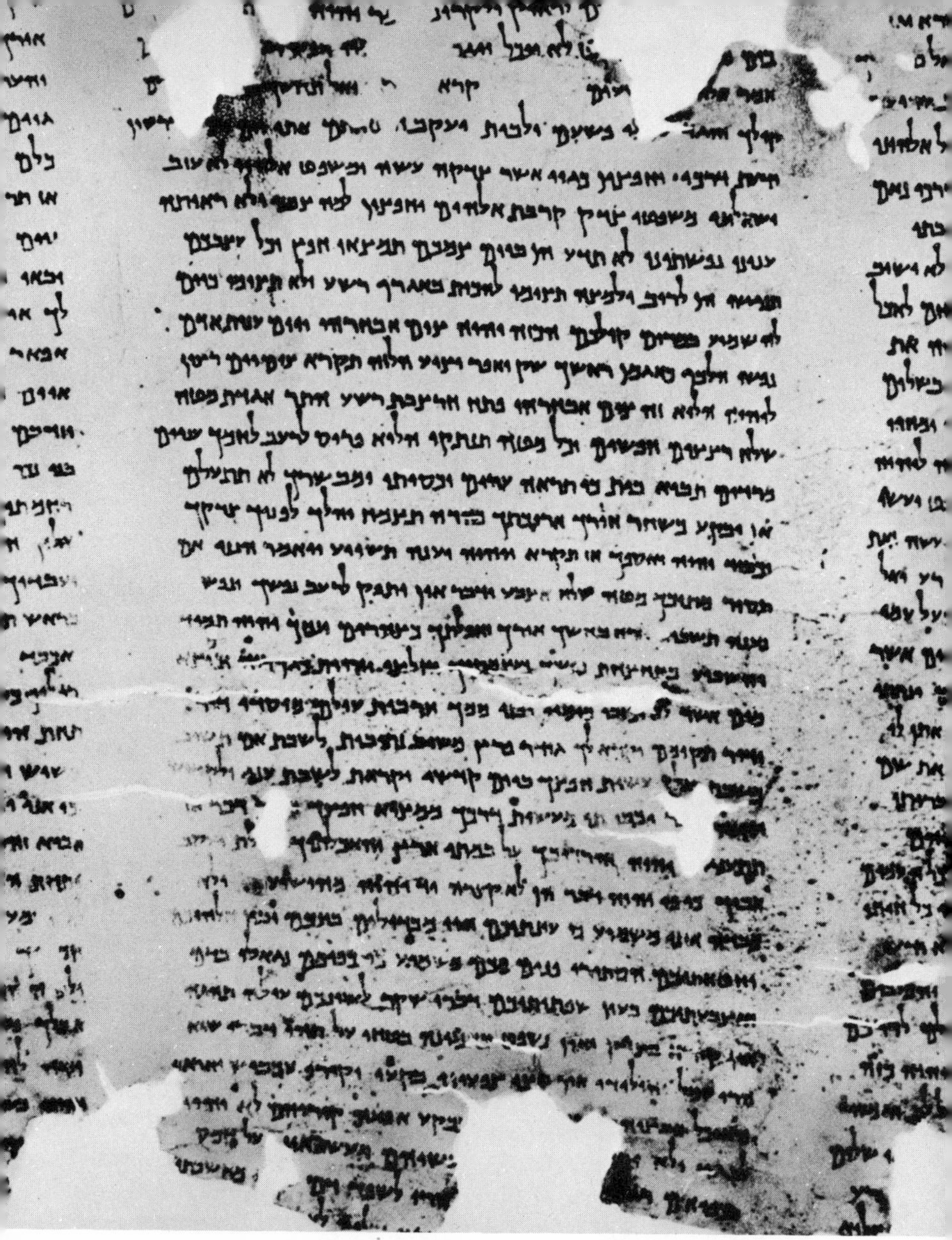

A fragment of the Isaiah scroll

acting as pro-tem government during the transition to Israeli statehood would wish to buy them for the Hebrew University. But the Agency had moved from Jerusalem to Tel Aviv. Telephone, mail and bus service between the two cities was disrupted. Dr. Sukenik searched for persons in Jerusalem who might be able to reach the proper officials.

He applied to his bank for a loan but was refused because of the uncertainty of war conditions.

As each day went by he grew more and more anxious. Sleepless during the nights, he would frequently get out of bed to pore over the scrolls in his library. He copied parts of Isaiah, hardly daring to believe the words in front of him. If he was right, and the script of the scrolls was that of the first or second century B.C., then this scroll of Isaiah was the oldest handwritten Bible book in the world.

Throughout the centuries before the invention of printing, both Jewish and Christian scribes had copied Bible books as the old ones wore out. In such hand-copying it was only natural that mistakes should occur. A scribe might be careless, impatient, or even feel his own words improved the original. No Bible, whether it was the one used by Jews or by different Christian faiths, could be called authentic in the sense that its wording was exactly the same as an Old Testament book when first written.

The major substance of Old Testament books of different Bibles was the same, of course. The stories of King David or of Ruth and Naomi were the stories both Jews and Christians knew.

The oldest version of the Old Testament was the Septuagint, or the "Seventy," so-called because according to legend some seventy scholars had worked on it. It was written in the third century B.C. Ptolemy II of Egypt, who valued Jewish learning, had brought the seventy (actually seventy-two) scholars to Alexandria and set them the task of translating the Hebrew Bible into Greek.

This Septuagint became the Bible of Greek-speaking Jews, and, in later centuries, the Old Testament of Greek-speaking Christians. As time went on translations of it were made into many different languages. But the original Septuagint does not exist. It disappeared long ago. The best-known, earliest copies are the one in the Vatican Library, dated about A.D. 350, and the one in the British Museum from the fifth century A.D.

In the seventh century A.D., Jewish scholars met to standardize and correct mistakes that had crept into the copying of the Hebrew-language Bible. The scribes were scattered all over Europe, and slight differences of wording made it necessary to set up one semi-official edition for all. The resulting Hebrew edition was called the Masoretic text, and the oldest copy dates from the tenth century.

Neither Christian nor Jew could be certain how closely the wording of his Old Testament followed the original books of the ancients—books lost in the mists of thousands of years.

This scroll of Isaiah, then, could be of the utmost importance to Bible scholars, as well as to linguists, historians, archaeologists and paleographers. Would this

Isaiah scroll confirm the wording of the Masoretic text or the Septuagint? Or would its text differ from both? If Dr. Sukenik was right, this scroll was older than any known copy in existence.

The explosion of bombs and the sound of gunfire had changed from a sporadic to an almost constant detonation outside Dr. Sukenik's study windows, but he tried to concentrate. He grew desperate in his search for money. He had no idea what Kiraz and the Metropolitan would ask in payment, but he thought if he could give them two thousand English pounds, about six thousand dollars, they would be satisfied. It was no great sum for such treasures as these scrolls, but he was unable to raise it.

The University did not have such funds. Only the Jewish Agency could supply the money, and it was in the difficult situation of providing some form of government for a nation that would not be a nation until the British mandate was over, while at the same time preparing for war. Conditions were chaotic. Dr. Sukenik got in touch with Kiraz, who agreed to extend the deadline until February 6.

On the very last day Dr. Sukenik was told that the director of the literary institution of the Jewish Agency was in Jerusalem. He was the man to see. An appointment was made, but for some reason this official was not able to keep it.

Dr. Sukenik could do no more. The Jewish Agency headquarters at the moment were in Tel Aviv, and transportation to and from that city was limited to the military. He had had the scrolls ten days; he could not have another extension. He must return the scrolls to Kiraz and try, somehow, to keep negotiations alive for a while longer. As he walked up the Y.M.C.A. steps he scarcely noticed the Arabs around him. He felt despair and a sense of foreboding.

Kiraz took the scrolls and asked immediately: "How much?" Dr. Sukenik could only pretend to bargain and play for time. What was the Metropolitan's asking price? Neither Kiraz nor Sukenik could name an amount. Another meeting was set for the following week, but Dr. Sukenik had the feeling his chance had been missed. He saw the Isaiah scroll go out of his hands with a sense of agonizing loss.

He was right. A letter arrived stating that the Metropolitan had decided not to sell. Dr. Sukenik wrote in his diary: "Thus the Jewish people have lost a priceless heritage."

It was some consolation to him to find that the third scroll from the Bethlehem dealer was also a book of Isaiah. However, in contrast to the Metropolitan's, it was not well preserved. Decomposition of the leather had produced a sticky substance over the words, making it difficult to read. Furthermore, it was incomplete, being only a part of the last third of the book, with some fragments from the middle.

CHAPTER III

THE METROPOLITAN broke off negotiations with Dr. Sukenik because another monk of St. Mark's, Brother Sowmy, suggested he get in touch with the American School of Oriental Research, instead. Dr. Sukenik's interest in the scrolls had given the Metropolitan increased hope they were valuable. The money potential of a sale through the help of Americans might be greater than to Dr. Sukenik.

The American School was in the Arab Husseini Quarter, outside the walls of the Old City. From the School it was possible to reach some of the gates of the Old City without going through British military zones, although Arab guards at the gates also demanded passes both in and out. Communication between the monastery inside the walls and the School outside was possible by telephone—when the lines weren't cut.

So it was that on February 18, 1948, Brother Sowmy

telephoned the School. He had already found out that Dr. Millar Burrows, the director, was away on a two-week trip to Baghdad, and he asked for Dr. William H. Brownlee. Brownlee was not in the building at the moment, but Dr. John C. Trever came to the phone.

Brother Sowmy said he was calling from St. Mark's; that he was the monastery librarian; that in cataloguing their collection of rare books he had come across some scrolls in ancient Hebrew, which had been in the monastery for about forty years. He wondered if Dr. Trever would look them over and tell him something about them —for the purposes of cataloguing.

Trever was curious. How could Syrian monks have scrolls of archaic Hebrew in their library? Yes, he told Brother Sowmy, he'd like to see them but he had no pass to go into the Old City. Privately, he also thought he had no relish for chancing bombs and bullets to see scrolls that might not be very old, after all.

The monk readily agreed to come to the School with the scrolls at two-thirty the next afternoon, and John Trever went back to other studies, putting the conversation out of his mind.

Both he and Brownlee were students at the School on fellowships, a very special privilege accorded to graduate Bible scholars or young archaeologists. Dr. Burrows was their professor and director, and ordinarily such a matter as Brother Sowmy's telephone call would have been referred to him, but Trever was acting director in Burrows' absence, and so it was his responsibility. He had also to cope with the difficult problems of getting food for

|47

The American School of Oriental Research

the School during those days of war, and of trying to restore electricity every time it was shut off. The service was poor and unreliable.

On the next day, however, the lights did go on, and so, since heating oil was scarce, Trever tried to warm one room for his expected guest by keeping a small hot plate going. At two-thirty a taxi arrived bringing Brother

Sowmy, accompanied by his brother Ibrahim. The first thing the monk did upon entering the room was to declare it too hot and stuffy and open the windows! Trever, shivering, realized that the monastery was never heated and that Brother Sowmy was, therefore, very warmly dressed.

He carried a leather satchel. Opening it, he lifted out a thin bundle wrapped in Arabic newspapers, unwound the papers and handed Trever a brittle, cream-colored scroll. The American just had time to look at a few words on the inside end of this scroll and note, with surprise, an unfamiliar Hebrew script, when Brother Sowmy handed him another, very large scroll.

They were in Trever's bedroom, and he took the larger scroll and carefully unwound it on the bed. As he looked at the script he became more and more astonished. He examined letters through a magnifying glass, and his bewilderment grew. He was accustomed to studying archaic Hebrew scripts, but this was different. His mind raced through memories of the writing of the oldest Hebrew Bible manuscripts he had ever seen—but they were no help.

His wife had recently sent him his color slides of the history of the Bible text, and now he turned to these. He thumbed through the slides, and suddenly stopped at one. This was of a small papyrus fragment called the Nash Papyrus, about three inches by five inches, inscribed with the Ten Commandments, which a noted scholar, Dr. W. F. Albright, had dated as having been written in the first or second centuries B.C. Trever compared the color-photograph slide of the Nash Papyrus with the scroll on the bed and saw, under the magnifying lens, that the "M" and the "K" were distinctly similar.

The implications were stunning, particularly to a young Bible scholar. Was it possible that this scroll would prove to be one of the oldest Hebrew manuscripts in the world? The tiny Nash Papyrus had been considered a documental find of the greatest importance, but here in this room were entire scrolls which might be equally old!

He tried hard not to show his excitement. He remembered a story of another discovery, of an ancient Greek manuscript, in a monastery. The eagerness of the discoverer had so alarmed the monks that the manuscript vanished into their library and was not seen again for fifteen years. Trever could not let that happen to the scrolls. He explained to Brother Sowmy that the study of such old manuscripts took a lot of time. Would the monk allow him to photograph a column of the scroll on the bed, so he could examine it at his leisure, more carefully?

Brother Sowmy agreed. Then Trever found himself frustrated. He was an excellent photographer, but the camera he needed was at the Palestine Museum where he had left it the day before. Controlling the shaking of his hand, he copied some lines from one section, the best he could do under the circumstances.

Then Brother Sowmy repeated his false story about the scrolls: they had been purchased forty years before by a former Metropolitan, not Mar Athanasius, from some Bedouins who had found them in a cave, sealed in jars. Not for some time did Trever learn the truth, and it was even later before he understood the reason for the fiction.

The Metropolitan had deliberately dated the monastery's ownership of the scrolls back forty years, before the British mandate, before the Palestine Department of Antiquities had any jurisdiction over such discoveries. In this way the personnel of the American School of Oriental Research, who operated carefully under the laws of the mandate, would have no reason to report the scrolls to the Department of Antiquities and no qualms over the Metropolitan's right to ownership.

As soon as the two Sowmys had left, taking the scrolls away in the satchel, Trever went in search of Brownlee. Together, the two studied the few lines Trever had copied from the scroll. They grew more and more excited. The way in which two words were used together—"by not"— was certainly uncommon, and sent them hurrying to a Hebrew dictionary and then to a Hebrew Bible, where they found that the book of Isaiah used those same two words in conjunction. With this as a lead they compared the reference in Isaiah with the lines from the scroll and found the passage was exactly the same.

There could be no question about it: the large scroll was Isaiah. And if the similarity of the script between it and the Nash Papyrus could be definitely established, then certainly this was the oldest copy of Isaiah in existence. The two young men tried hard to curb their enthusiasm, realizing how unlikely it was that an entire scroll could survive for two thousand years, and aware that older and better-trained scholars might be able to prove they were wrong.

John Trever could not believe the scroll was a fake. The next morning he determined to go to the monastery. He had no pass for the Old City, but a woman who was secretary to the American School and who could speak Arabic agreed to help him. They took a bus, not without misgivings on the part of Trever, since two buses had been bombed and thirteen people killed in the month of December.

At the Jaffa Gate they found the entrance heavily barricaded. Armed guards queried everyone, whether or not they had a pass. Though the secretary argued with them they were plainly suspicious of a man like Trever who did not look Arabic. Finally, however, the guard conducted them inside the Gate to the office of the Arab Emergency Committee. Trever could understand a little of what was said there, and realized they objected to giving him a pass because they suspected the American School of being friendly to, or harboring, Jews.

At last the official shrugged and stamped the pass. Trever took it thankfully, since it now meant he could go in and out as he pleased, and would have the right to visit the monastery. He walked along King David Street, passing a maze of tiny, branching passageways, turned into Christian Street and at last found himself in the Armenian Quarter where the monastery was located.

Brother Sowmy was surprised to see him so soon, but took him immediately to meet the Metropolitan. Over the inevitable coffee cups they made polite conversation; then Trever asked about the earlier Metropolitan who had purchased the scrolls. What was his name? What were the circumstances? Did the Metropolitan think the Bedouins might still have some of the jars?

The Metropolitan and Brother Sowmy spoke to each other in Arabic, then Brother Sowmy explained that Mar Athanasius had been in charge of the monastery for only fourteen months and could not know all the circumstances, but they would try to reach the Bedouins and see if any jars had been kept.

In turn, Trever was questioned. Had he found out how old the scrolls were? The American felt it was much too early to speak of his own conviction as to their antiquity, and he could only say, quite honestly, that it would take much more time, and that many scholars would have to study them. He asked that he be allowed to photograph all the scrolls. Once the columns of texts were photographed they could be studied from the prints. Pictures could be seen by more scholars, and the scrolls would not have to be handled so much and risk being damaged.

When Trever saw the Metropolitan was reluctant to give this permission, he told them about the Greek manuscript that had also been discovered in a monastery. Only after that manuscript had been photographed, and the photographs circulated to many scholars so they could vouch for its antiquity, had the British government paid five hundred thousand dollars for it in 1933. The Metropolitan heard the account, and was obviously very much impressed by the figure. He agreed to have the scrolls brought to the School the next morning.

Before he left, Trever once again looked at the large Isaiah scroll. He was immediately struck by the fact that

|53

corrections had been made in it. After the original scribe had finished, others had made insertions to correct words or letters. One of the corrections had obviously been made by a skilled penman, while another was made by a much clumsier hand. To the American this was additional proof that the scroll was not a fake.

He could imagine a modern forger, with some knowledge of the ancient script, going to the enormous amount of trouble it would take to get aged leather and inscribing a book of Isaiah on it, but he found it impossible to believe a forger would be so clever as to supply himself with misspelled words and then have someone else correct them!

The next day brought its own problems. When the scrolls arrived, Trever would have liked to photograph each column separately, but he did not have enough film. Normal photographic supplies from outside Palestine had been almost cut off because of the undeclared war raging in the country. He would have to put several columns on a single sheet of film, and he could only get all fifty-four columns of the Isaiah scroll—if he made not one single mistake and ruined not one sheet of film.

He ushered the Metropolitan and Brother Sowmy downstairs to the basement laboratory and showed them his preparations: camera and floodlight and the drawing board upon which he laid the scroll. For the actual pictures the scroll would have to be stretched out on the floor, upon heavy wrapping paper. All was ready—except for one thing. The night before, a battle had raged just to the north of the school and, as usual, the electric lines had been cut. Repairmen were working on them and had promised the current would soon be restored, but Trever was nervous.

The Metropolitan had been reluctantly persuaded to permit the scrolls to be photographed; he might change his mind if there were delays. Outside the basement window Trever saw the repairmen working. It was a blessing to him when Brother Sowmy whispered that the ceremony of coffee had obviously been forgotten, and Trever could stall a little longer while Brownlee went to the kitchen for the refreshments.

But at last the coffee-drinking was over and the moment had come. Trever focused the camera, Brownlee flicked the switch, the lights went on—and immediately flickered out again. The two Americans exchanged a glance and quickly shifted the scroll over to where sunlight coming in through the window made one patch of light. The weak February sunshine was no substitute for the powerful floodlight, but it would have to do. Just as they got into the new position, the electric light flashed on again, and this time the current remained steady. The lines had been fixed.

Brownlee and Trever worked feverishly, yet carefully, with the feeling they must take advantage of the opportunity, yet fearful of spoiling even one sheet of their precious film. Even at that, there was only enough for the one scroll. Their guests seemed interested in the photographic process and watched with curiosity when Scotch tape was applied to the back of the scroll in places where cracks were threatening to become breaks.

When the Isaiah scroll was finally on film and the

Metropolitan and Brother Sowmy had departed, both Trever and Brownlee were exhausted. Yet all that evening they worked in the darkroom to develop the film; by midnight they had twelve sheets hanging up to dry, and they went to bed.

The next day was Sunday, a day that always seemed particularly favored by both Arabs and Jews for fighting. Explosions rocked Jerusalem; two trucks full of explosives had been timed to go off on Ben Yehudi Street, killing forty-nine people. But war outside could not stop the work inside the School. Trever managed somehow to find more film, and he and Brownlee began the task of photographing the next two scrolls, in between dashes to the darkroom to develop more pictures of the Isaiah scroll.

Both the other two scrolls were cream colored and of the same texture of leather, and when their cracks had been backed with tape so they could be unrolled and laid flat it could be seen they were actually one scroll, fitting together where the ancient sewing of two sections had worn away. There was no time to try to read it; they just labeled it Jerusalem Scroll I, and began photographing.

Monday morning, Trever was committed to a visit to Jericho, but by afternoon he was back in the laboratory. Now the films were all dry and the two men could see, with joy, that the pictures of the Isaiah scroll, both in color and black and white, were perfect. They wanted to take color shots of the Jerusalem I, and photograph a smaller, darker scroll, Jerusalem II, and the scrolls had to be back at the monastery the following day. Neither

Trever nor Brownlee had time to congratulate themselves on their good photography. They were much too busy.

Almost the first question the Metropolitan asked, the next day at St. Mark's, was how old the scrolls were, but again Trever refused to commit himself. He assured Mar Athanasius that the scrolls would be shown to Dr. Millar Burrows when he returned, and that he would keep the Metropolitan informed of whatever progress he and Brownlee made in their studies.

One scroll remained untouched. It was so tightly rolled and so stuck together that Trever urged that it be sent to America where it could be opened by experts. He would not attempt it himself, because he might damage it. The Metropolitan said nothing to this, but his usual reserve had given way to a warm reception. When Trever and Brownlee left they felt much had been accomplished. They did not have the scrolls but they had photographs to read and study, and were sure of a welcome at the monastery.

More than one print was made from the same film, so Trever could send a few sample photographs to Dr. Albright, Professor of Semitic Languages at Johns Hopkins University in the United States, who had published an analysis of the Nash Papyrus. His letter to Albright stated his hopes that the script of the Isaiah scroll was as old as the Nash Papyrus, which would make it the oldest Bible document yet discovered.

While Trever went on developing the film of the other scrolls and Brownlee concentrated on reading the prints of Jerusalem Scroll II, they took time out to discuss the publication of the photographs. Although none of the color or black-and-white films had been spoiled, it was realized that they were not good enough to reproduce well in print. What was needed for better pictures were larger film sheets—13 by 18 centimeters—and where could they be found?

The logical place was not the shops, which were suffering scarcities, but the Palestine Archaeological Museum. This splendid museum was a gift from John D. Rockefeller, Jr., and was well financed by a trust fund; if anyone had film it would be the office of the Palestine Department of Antiquities in the museum. Trever went to pay a call on the Director, Mr. R. W. Hamilton.

Since Trever told him the story as he knew it, of scrolls owned by the monastery for forty years, Mr. Hamilton was personally interested but not officially so, since he had no jurisdiction over them. He listened, and looked at the photographs, but not being a paleographer he had no expert knowledge of the age of the scripts. He wished Trever success—but he had no film to give him.

Ever since Trever's first meeting with Brother Sowmy, he and Brownlee had lived in a state of emotional tension. The afternoon had been a severe disappointment, but that evening their spirits swung to high excitement when Brownlee, in studying the Jerusalem Scroll II, discovered it was a commentary on the Book of Habakkuk.

A sentence from the Old Testament Habakkuk would be followed by an interpretation by an unknown author. For example, they found these words from Habakkuk:

58|

The Palestine Archaeological Museum

"For, lo, I raise up the Chaldeans, that bitter and hasty nation," and the scroll added: "Its hidden interpretation refers to the Kittim, who are swift and valiant in battle to destroy mighty rulers."

Brownlee's quick reading, catching a familiar quotation here and there, would have to be followed by an intensive study.

Dr. Burrows returned, to be greeted by two almost incoherent students. He listened to their story, but being more used to disappointments, and trained to a scientific skepticism, he withheld any premature enthusiasm until he had had a chance to see the scrolls for himself. This he did the next day at the monastery; after a few days of studying the script from the photographs he, too, was convinced of their two-thousand-year age and was as enthusiastic as Trever and Brownlee.

It was decided that almost all the classes Dr. Burrows had been giving the two young men be dropped in favor of studying the scrolls. The director could see that Trever and Brownlee had already learned a great deal about the research of old manuscripts since they had first looked at the scrolls. John Trever had come to Jerusalem with little or no previous experience in ancient scripts, but he was learning fast.

The step-by-step procedure in studying such scrolls was rarely that—a step at a time. The investigations were more likely to concern themselves with "who wrote?" and "when written?" all at the same time. The questions to be asked and answered were: Was the manuscript genuine? If so, how old? In what language was it written? In what age or period of the language had that particular script been used? What were its contents? If religious, how did they compare with other religious texts, and if they were not religious, were they purely literary? Could the age of the scroll be determined from its contents? If so, would the contents throw further light upon the history of the age in which it was written?

The conditions of the leather and ink were indications of great age. The script dated the scrolls in the first century. Another clue to the dating was the reference to the enemy as Kittim. Dr. Burrows believed it could be a veiled way of saying "Romans." Leather, ink and script were all indications the scrolls were genuine. The fact that two of the scrolls were not books of the Bible was further proof. A forger could copy an Old Testament book, but he could not copy something unknown, as was the Habakkuk Commentary.

The first reading of any of the scrolls was a quick sampling to determine what it was; then came the detailed word-for-word study, at best a difficult task. Even when that had been done, Dr. Burrows cautioned, a few of the questions would be answered conclusively by their individual efforts alone. It was vital to scholarly research that the photographs be published as widely as possible. Only from the debates and discussions by many scholars all over the world would the most accurate answers eventually emerge.

Although Dr. Burrows even at this stage already had an idea of when the scrolls had been written, it was too early to project his theory.

Trever's photographic work proceeded along with his studies. Some old, out-of-date film of the right size was finally obtained by scrounging through the shops, and more prints were made. Trever was also meticulous in keeping his appointments with the Metropolitan, and on March 5 he went to the monastery to make a report on the progress of the filming. He also wanted to urge that the scrolls be removed from the Old City for safety. In May the British would withdraw; the tempo of the war was increasing, and the monastery was as vulnerable a target for a bomb as any other building. The evidence was all around them. Inside and outside the City houses and shops had been reduced to rubble.

Trever informed the Metropolitan that all Americans had been asked to leave Jerusalem and that the School was even now in the process of packing up. The Metropolitan was alarmed at this news. He urged Trever to stay, saying there was a special need for him to remain because of the scrolls. When Trever showed his puzzlement, Mar Athanasius turned to Brother Sowmy and said something in Arabic.

Then Brother Sowmy, for the first time, told Trever the true story of the scrolls: how they had not been in the monastery for forty years but had been purchased only months before from the Bedouins. The Syrians knew where the cave was, and they wanted Trever to stay on and make an expedition to the caves to get the jar and other things that Father Yusif had seen there.

Trever was jolted. The story seemed fantastic. He could not promise anything until he talked to Dr. Burrows. He left the monastery as quickly as he could to return to the

School and tell Burrows of this new development. Burrows' reaction, too, was one of amazement. He agreed it was highly important to try to reach the cave, but not without the knowledge and permission of the Department of Antiquities.

Before this was applied for, a way must be found to the cave. The general area around the north end of the Dead Sea, in the vicinity of where Father Yusif said the cave was located, was highly dangerous. A Jewish company had a potash plant there. Its convoys of trucks attracted Arab ambushes, and the roads were apt to be raked with gunfire at the sight of any car. While Trever was considering another route, he received an air letter dated March 15, from Dr. Albright in America. It read in part:

"My heartiest congratulations on the greatest manuscript discovery of modern times! There is no doubt in my mind that the script is more archaic than that of the Nash Papyrus . . . I should prefer a date around 100 B.C.! . . . What an absolutely incredible find! And there can happily not be the slightest doubt in the world about the genuineness of the manuscript."

Though Dr. Burrows had had no doubts about either the age or authenticity of the scrolls, it was good to have this view confirmed by another eminent scholar. The time had come now to tell the Metropolitan of the true importance of the scrolls, and to persuade him to send them to a place of safety.

When the Metropolitan heard the good news, his dignity kept him from showing more than gratification, but —as he was to recount later—as soon as Brownlee and

Trever left, he went to his chapel to unburden his emotions and give thanks. Not long afterward he let Brother Sowmy take the four scrolls to Beirut, Lebanon, where they were deposited in a bank vault.

John Trever called upon Mr. Hamilton for permission to excavate the cave, but completely forgot to tell him the cave had been discovered recently—not forty years ago. The omission was unintentional. Trever's mind was wholly occupied at that moment with the difficulties of reaching the cave, with the pressure of having so little time left to accomplish anything, and on the delicate position of the American School in relation both to the Department of Antiquities and to the Syrians. He confided in Mr. Hamilton that the Metropolitan did not want the Department informed about the cave, but the School could not proceed without legal permission. Hamilton, still thinking the scrolls were no concern of his, assured Trever he understood the need to be diplomatic in dealing with the Syrians, and he would say nothing to them about the scrolls. The cave was a different matter. Trever was given permission to visit and photograph its contents, but not to disturb whatever was there without further checking with Hamilton.

Any misunderstanding between the Department and the American School was purely accidental, the result of the pressure of time on Trever and the almost frenzied need to accomplish as much as possible with the scrolls and the cave before the School personnel would be forced to leave.

But the arrangements to visit the cave fell through. It was too dangerous an undertaking and the time too short. An agreement was reached with the Metropolitan for the American School to publish the photographs in America, and then the School was temporarily closed. Brownlee left first, then Dr. Burrows, and on April 5 John Trever took a plane to Lebanon.

When the British withdrew all troops before midnight on May 14, the establishment of the State of Israel was proclaimed, and full-scale hostilities broke out, with tanks, planes, bombs and guns, in spite of efforts at a truce by the United Nations. But all the photographs were safe in America, and the scrolls were soon to follow them.

St. Mark's monastery was exposed to the fire of both Arabs and Israelis. On May 16 Brother Sowmy was killed in the monastery courtyard by a stray bullet.

The Metropolitan's church superiors knew about the scrolls, and this may have played a part in a change for him. In October of 1948 the Syrian Patriarch designated Mar Athanasius as Apostolic Delegate to the United Nations and Canada. He was to leave as soon as possible. His duties were to help build up the Syrian churches in America and to collect money and supplies to send back to Palestine and Jordan, since many of the Syrian congregation were now war refugees.

Throughout October and November Mar Athanasius made his preparations. By the end of the year he would take ship for America, stopping first in Lebanon to pick up the scrolls.

Meanwhile there was another man in Jordan who, had he known, would have been intensely interested in the departure of the Metropolitan and would certainly have forbidden him to take the scrolls away.

CHAPTER IV

THE END OF THE BRITISH MANDATE and the birth of Israel brought about the creation of the Hashemite Kingdom of Jordan. The original name was the Hashemite Kingdom of Jordan and Palestine, since the Arabs did not recognize Israel's claim to any part of that country, but eventually it became just Jordan. In the latter part of the year the boundaries between Israel and Jordan were not clearly defined; battles moved them this way and that; a street inside Jerusalem might be taken today and lost tomorrow. In general, though, it could be said that the Old City and everything east of it was in Jordanian hands. This included the Palestine Museum, the Jordan valley and the Dead Sea area.

The incorporation of Arab Palestine with Jordan in the Hashemite Kingdom of Jordan was not formally proclaimed until December 13, 1948, but long before that the military and some offices of government had begun functioning.

There was no longer a Palestine Department of Antiquities, but a Jordanian Department, which considered itself the heir to what the previous organization had accomplished, as well as to such buildings as the Museum and its archaeological treasures. Hamilton resigned when the British left, and his assistant, G. Lankester Harding —another Englishman—took his place.

Harding had offices both in the Palestine Museum and in Amman, the official capital of Jordan. It lay northeast of the Dead Sea and even farther northeast of Jerusalem. On this November day in 1948 Harding sat at his desk in Amman, staring at a copy of the April *Bulletin of the American Schools of Oriental Research,* and at an article in it by Dr. Albright on the finding of the Dead Sea scrolls.

Harding was shocked. Since the war postal communications were in chaos. His mail arrived seldom and then extremely late. It had taken seven months for this publication to reach him, and it was his first knowledge of the existence of the scrolls.

It seemed incredible to him that such a momentous manuscript discovery should have been made in the Dead Sea area and that the Department of Antiquities should have known nothing about it. Later he would learn that Hamilton had been aware of the find and that it had been an unfortunate chain of circumstances that had kept Hamilton from the thought of legally acquiring them. He would in time realize that it was the turmoil of war— and the Metropolitan's secrecy—that had permitted the scrolls to be taken out of the country.

But at this moment he was angry. He placed a telephone call to Joseph Saad, a young Jordanian who was Secretary and Curator of the Palestine Museum in Jerusalem, which was under Harding's jurisdiction. While the call was being put through he waited restlessly—a tall, lean, soft-spoken man who was ordinarily very patient and rarely upset. When he smiled, slow crinkles formed around his blue eyes, but he was not smiling now.

His call came through. Harding told Saad about the article and the discovery of the scrolls. "Did you know anything about these?" he asked.

"No, nothing at all," came Saad's startled reply.

"Will you try to find out about them, in Jerusalem?" Harding asked.

Joseph Saad was at a loss. "But how am I going to find out anything? Give me a clue." He was hoping the article had mentioned the specific tribe of Bedouins and who had handled the sale for them.

Harding had no such clues. When he hung up he knew he must go to Jerusalem to consult his friend, Father Roland de Vaux. After an hour's drive he reached the place where the Jordan River ran beneath the road bridge to empty into the Dead Sea. Here he stopped briefly. He was on the east-west highway which led across the valley, up through the hills to Jerusalem. On his left were the great blue salt lake and the desert plains around it.

This was the bleached land of wilderness, strewn with boulders or rubble, cut with rocky ravines, scorched by the sun in summer and pounded by short, torrential rains in the winter.

As Harding sat in the car facing the road to Jerusalem

his eyes traveled from the salt sea across the plain to the mountains. The colors were amazing. As light and shadow shifted across the rocky face of the ridge, pinks and reds, purple and tawny-yellow shades came into prominence or faded into gray. The bold heights and the brilliant colors had always delighted him, but today his mind was on something else. He studied the lower mountain slopes. Somewhere, perhaps hidden in those slopes, was the cave. It would have to be found.

He started his car again and drove on to Jerusalem to the French Dominican Bible and Archaeological School. There he found Father de Vaux.

Probably no two men ever presented a greater contrast. Harding was a reserved Englishman, Father de Vaux the most Gallic of Frenchmen, volatile, voluble, quick to laugh and quick to frown. Beside the tall Harding, de Vaux seemed short, though he was average height. Where the Englishman was deliberate in his movements, the Frenchman was brisk and full of expressive gestures. He pulled at his beard and his sparse gray hair when he was upset, and spoke with his hands as eloquently as with his mouth. One was Protestant, the other a Catholic priest.

The two men had great respect for each other, based on long acquaintance and knowledge of each other's abilities. Harding was a most able administrator and archaeologist; de Vaux was unquestionably one of the leading Bible scholars and archaeologists of the Middle East.

He, too, had just read about the scrolls. He had been away from Jerusalem when van der Ploeg, residing at the Dominican School, had looked at the scrolls, and had not known about the incident. He was astonished to find Harding knew no more than he did. Whatever the reasons were, it was vital that both the cave and the Bedouins be found. Harding decided that Joseph Saad, as a Jordanian whose connection with the Department of Antiquities was not widely known, would be the best choice for making inquiries. The scrolls had obviously been sold illicitly by the Bedouins; they would not be apt to talk to Harding, who had long worked in the Department.

The two archaeologists walked over to the Palestine Museum to ask the young man's help. Unhesitatingly Joseph Saad agreed, although he knew what possible dangers he faced. He must travel to Bethlehem, along roads which at one moment might be safely behind the battle-lines and the next squarely within them. A frightened merchant or a Bedouin anxious to escape suspicion or punishment for his part in the sale of the scrolls was likely to make trouble. War bred lawlessness, and although Harding gave Joseph Saad authority to promise that persons involved would *not* be punished, would they believe him?

Harding did not want the men penalized. He wanted to know if there were more scrolls still unsold, and the whereabouts of the cave. Even with all his experience in the desert he might never find the cave on his own; the Judaean mountains stretched for miles from north to south along the Dead Sea. His best chance was to persuade the Bedouins it was safe to talk.

Although Bethlehem has historic significance throughout the Christian world, it has remained a small village. Around the Church of the Nativity there had grown up a maze of short, narrow streets where shopkeepers sold their wares to tourists, but the rest was like the ordinary Arab village. The shy Bedouin tribes felt at home in Bethlehem when they visited there. They could pitch their tents and keep their herds on its outskirts as their ancestors had done before them.

Word traveled swiftly in a place that size. Joseph Saad came to Bethlehem because Professor Albright in his article had written of an unnamed Bethlehem merchant, but he soon realized that suspicion walked ahead of him. No one would say a word about the scrolls. No one would give him the name of the dealer. He tried to be discreet and casual as he wandered through the streets, but any mention of the scrolls was met with silence.

Frustrated, he returned to Jerusalem. He went next to the American School of Oriental Research. Dr. O. R. Sellers had succeeded Millar Burrows as Director, and knew that the American School had had dealings with St. Mark's monastery. Dr. Sellers agreed to go with Saad to see the monks.

The Metropolitan had already left Lebanon and was in the United States; in his absence the other monks were evasive. They did reveal the name of George Shaya, and an appointment was made to meet him at the monastery the next day.

Once more Joseph Saad and Dr. Sellers made the perilous journey through gunfire to the monastery, but, although George Shaya admitted that he had made an expedition to the cave, he refused to reveal its whereabouts. By chance, the elderly Father Yusif, who had investigated the cave at the Metropolitan's request, walked by them, and Joseph Saad, on impulse, turned to him and asked the whereabouts of the cave.

Before George Shaya could stop him the old monk said just enough to give Saad a general idea of the cave's location. It was on the west side of the Dead Sea, in the Judaean mountains, south of the main road to Jerusalem, but no more than six miles south.

George Shaya was offered money to lead an expedition to the cave, but although he wavered between yes and no for a while, he eventually refused.

After this last futile attempt to enlist Shaya's help Joseph Saad resolved to seek some other way of finding the cave. The daily trips to the monastery were exhausting, and his efforts there seemed to have come to a dead end.

As usual, returning to the Palestine Museum that day raised Saad's spirits a little. In 1927 John D. Rockefeller had donated one million dollars for the building, and another million in the form of an endowment fund, the income from which was to be used for the maintenance of the museum and for purchases. It was a beautiful building. From the high center two flat-roofed wings stretched out like arms. It was modern, yet designed so that it would be harmonious with the surrounding buildings of Jerusalem. The arched windows, the flower gardens, the lawns and olive trees made it an oasis of quiet loveliness.

Saad pushed open the bronze doors.

Immediately he was faced with another problem. The Museum had been turned into a military post. A whole brigade of the Arab Legion was quartered there. Instead of the quiet properly belonging to a museum, there was the constant thump of soldiers' boots, the clatter of their arms and ammunition, the urgent shout of orders. Although the treasures of the Museum were now buried in the vaults below, the curator had to use all his diplomacy to keep the soldiers from defacing the white walls, or using sharp bayonets to scratch idle signs on the paneled wood doors.

Passing a group of them in one of the exhibition rooms he smiled and spoke to Captain Akkash el-Zebn. He noticed how striking his red-and-white headdress looked against the background of white wall.

The Arab Legion! Joseph Saad stopped. Something had occurred to him. Legionnaires were recruited from desert tribes and trained in desert police work. They knew the land around the Dead Sea as well as any Bedouin herdsman. If anyone could pick out one cave among the hundreds that honeycombed the Judaean mountains, a man like Captain Akkash could.

Immediately Joseph Saad went looking for the Legion commander, Major-General Lash. By strange coincidence, the Major-General had been discussing the mystery of the cave with a Belgian United Nations observer, Captain Lippens, and they had already telephoned to Harding, who had enthusiastically endorsed their idea of a search.

It was understood that if the cave were found nothing in it was to be touched until the archaeologists, Harding and de Vaux, could get there to supervise the work.

With the information that Joseph Saad and Dr. Sellers had gotten from Father Yusif, a search party consisting of Captain Lippens, Captain Akkash el-Zebn and an English Legion officer, Brigadier Ashton, set out on January 25. On January 28 there came a triumphant phone call to Harding: the cave had been found.

At least, *a* cave had been found which might be the one. Besides a natural entrance, high up, another hole had been made at foot level. The ground in front had been disturbed and a pile of debris dumped there.

Immediately Harding set out from Amman. When he came to the east-west road to Jerusalem he crossed the Jordan River and then carefully eased his old car off the road into the trackless wasteland. The guidesign he had been given to look for was the high, sandy plateau of Khirbet Qumran, jutting out from the mountainside. He knew this landmark and maneuvered the car around boulders, up and down gullies, bouncing over stones and ridges of earth.

His way was diagonal; the mountains and the road made the other two sides of the triangle, and his goal was the plateau.

As he neared it he saw the figures of Captain Lippens and Captain Akkash, waving to him from above. He got the car as close as he could and then walked, climbing the steep rise to the top of Khirbet Qumran with the practiced ease of an outdoor man.

74

The captains met him and led him off to the right, climbing farther up the mountainside. Finally they reached the entrance of a cave.

Harding was disappointed. True, there was a mound of debris at the lower entrance, which might have been scraped from inside and shoveled out during a search, but the cave was empty. A hole about the height of a boy's head seemed to be a natural opening, while another at ground level had been recently made. It was small, and Harding had to crawl in on hands and knees, but once inside he found he could stand upright. There was enough light from both openings so he could see fairly well, but there was nothing there. There were no jars, no scrolls, not even any visible pieces of leather lying about. Even the one jar mentioned by Father Yusif had vanished.

The Bedouins used caves as shelters from winter rains. The mound of earth outside might be just debris from several nights' camping. The broken pieces of pottery might be the Bedouins' own broken water jars.

Still, the quantity of pottery shards was intriguing. A large number of jars would have had to be broken to create so many fragments. Harding decided they warranted a scientific analysis. Brigadier Ashton agreed to remain on guard until Harding could return with de Vaux and the necessary archaeological equipment.

But it was winter and the next two weeks were ones of torrential rains, even of snow. Frustrated, Father de Vaux and Harding drove to the scene daily in their car but did not dare to venture off the paved road. The plain was impossible to cross, with water rushing down the gullies and carving new ravines through the sand and under rocks. Brigadier Ashton and the Arab Legion men were forced to resume their normal duties.

It was not until February 15 that the rains stopped and the two archaeologists, with Arab helpers, were able to make their way to the cave.

By noon of that day they were discouraged. They had worked all morning and found nothing but more broken pottery. Harding went down to the car to prepare lunch.

While he was gone de Vaux picked up a sliver of pottery and was about to place it with the others when his eyes spotted a tiny fragment clinging to it. For a second he stood motionless. He looked again. It was a piece of leather, and on it he could see three Hebrew letters!

He took a small notebook from his shirt pocket and carefully placed the tiny fragment between the pages. Harding was calling to him to come to lunch, and he went to the car, bursting with his discovery but keeping silent while he watched his friend unpack the baskets of food. They sat down. Harding took a drink of cold water from the thermos and then asked, casually, if anything more had been found.

Father de Vaux could wait no longer. His sandwich fell into his lap while he flipped open his notebook and displayed his find.

The sensation it caused was as great as he had hoped for. Harding looked at the fragment and at the letters on it with awed excitement. This *was* the cave. They could be almost certain of that.

And if there was one fragment there might be others,

overlooked by the Bedouins. The real work must now begin. After lunch they climbed to the cave once more, carrying supplies and instruments.

They studied the interior carefully. Cautiously they worked, first on their haunches; then, when they had cleared a sufficient area around them they lay flat on their stomachs, to work as close to the ground as possible. Inch by inch they turned over and sifted the earth covering the floor of the cave. They used pharmacy tweezers and soft, camel's-hair brushes to pick up and dust fragments, found buried or trodden into the earth. Some were no larger than half the length of a fingernail; some were so twisted they looked like dried leaves. As the afternoon wore on they brought in pressure oil lamps to light the cave.

It was tortuous work. Every half hour or so one of them would stagger outside to cough up the dust that had filled his lungs. After two days they were spitting up a little blood along with the dust. Their eyes were red with strain. The air inside the cave grew foul from the lamps.

The first night Father de Vaux had planned to sleep out, but a thunderstorm forced him inside the small tent which already sheltered Harding, a native workman and his dog.

They could laugh at such hardships. As long as the precious fragments were safe between glass slides nothing else mattered. The major scrolls and jars were gone, but it was exciting to know they were rescuing what was left. In addition to the scroll fragments, they were finding shreds of the linen which had been used as wrappings, and now they could feel sure the pottery shards at the cave's entrance had once been scroll jars. Their training and experience enabled them to estimate that at one time the cave had held forty or fifty of these jars.

What had happened to them? It was possible the Bedouins had more than the two already sold to Dr. Sukenik. But very likely most of the jars had broken of natural causes over a period of two thousand years. Perhaps there had been earthquakes, or hyenas and jackals may have used the cave as a lair, and knocked over some jars. The earth may have settled beneath others causing them to topple. Once the scrolls were exposed they would be eaten away by white ants, rats, the potassium in the soil, the urine of animals.

The two men asked each other questions neither could answer. What ancient Jews had placed these scrolls and jars in the cave? Why—in such a remote place? If the cave were a *genizah* it was no ordinary one, since it contained not only a book of Isaiah but entirely new religious works.

By now these were the questions the whole world was asking.

The Metropolitan had arrived in America to begin his new work. He had also re-established contact with the American Schools of Oriental Research. According to the contract drawn up in Jerusalem, the A.S.O.R. had exclusive rights to the publication of photographs, and to the study and publication of the texts for three years. The news of the "Dead Sea Scrolls" discovery was being headlined in newspapers and featured in magazines; Mar

Athanasius had high hopes that the scrolls could be sold for a considerable sum.

To add to the interest, the newspapers soon printed another startling revelation. Dr. Sukenik gave a press interview on the three scrolls from the same cave in the possession of the Hebrew University. It was the first either the Americans or Harding and de Vaux in Jerusalem had ever heard that other scrolls from the same source existed.

Not often does an archaeological discovery become a matter of extraordinary interest to ordinary people, but the "Dead Sea Scrolls" became a familiar term to nearly every newspaper reader. Their origin remained a mystery, but this only added to the excitement. Wild speculations began to appear in print.

Were they the work of John the Baptist, who had preached in the Wilderness by the Dead Sea? Were they early Christian manuscripts? Would all Bible texts be changed to conform with the translations of the Isaiah scroll? It was not only newspaper and magazine feature writers who indulged in guesses and fantasy. Even scholars were infected by the scroll fever and rushed into print with speculations and arguments.

There seemed to be as many scholars who refused to believe any evidence the scrolls were either old or authentic as there were who hailed them as genuine. The scoffers said they were either forgeries or only dated back to the Middle Ages. They had never been found in a cave. The whole story was nonsense. If these comments had come from uninformed people they might have been dismissed, but there were reputable scholars among the skeptics. They had to be answered. In spite of their many other duties, Drs. Burrows, Brownlee and Trever worked hard to prepare the scroll texts for publication.

Other problems had arisen. Anton Kiraz had lost his prosperous business in the Jerusalem battles, and was now putting forth a claim to half-ownership in the scrolls. He needed the money, but the Metropolitan denied his claim. Then there was the question of a box of scroll fragments that the Metropolitan showed to Trever for the first time.

Mar Athanasius stated he had had them since 1947, but Trever had reason to believe they had been taken from the cave, by Shaya or the Bedouins, in November, 1948, just before the Metropolitan left Jerusalem. Legal rights to those fragments depended largely on exactly when they had been acquired. The scrolls fell under the authority of the Palestinian Department of Antiquities— but that organization was now defunct and had no legal status. The box of fragments, however, had apparently been taken from the cave after the new Jordanian Department had begun functioning. The new department had jurisdiction over the Dead Sea area—and its legal status was beyond question.

The legal points were delicate ones. Trever urged Mar Athanasius to return the fragments to Jordan, and thus avoid a dispute with the Jordanian Department of Antiquities. He drafted a letter for him to the Department, reporting the acquisition of the fragments, and promising to return them to Jordan, but requesting permission to publish the photographs Trever had just taken of them. The Metropolitan signed the letter, it was mailed, and the Jordanian Department of Antiquities granted the permission regarding the photographs. They were published, but the Metropolitan did not keep his promise to send back the fragments.

In the meanwhile, in Jordan, Harding and Father de Vaux were continuing their work. Finding the cave was the first step in unraveling the puzzle of when the-scrolls had come into existence, and why they had been hidden in the cave. It seemed possible that the scribes who had copied them had lived somewhere near the cave, but the two men knew of no ancient Jewish town or settlement in that area.

They hoped for clues from the eventual full publication of the texts in Israel and America. But the first thing was to take the fragments they had found, now carefully sheltered between glass slides, and the pottery and linen scraps that had been on the floor of the cave to the Palestine Museum in Jerusalem. The next step was to try again to find the Bedouins for any further information and to see whether they had still more scrolls to sell.

Harding and Joseph Saad went to St. Mark's monastery. The monks recalled that the Metropolitan had dealt with some merchant, but they did not know his name. The trail seemed at an end. Father Yusif escorted Harding and Saad to the monastery gate. They asked him to contact them if he heard any more from the Bedouins or about any scroll fragments for sale.

Out of the corner of his eye Harding noticed that an Arab woman had paused to listen to their conversation. She started to walk on, hesitated, then turned back. When she looked directly at him, Harding smiled. Slowly she crossed the street, came close to him and whispered: was he interested in that cave? Her husband, Jabra, had gone there a year ago. He had been with George Shaya, had helped in the clearing out of the cave and had been rewarded with a big piece of leather. He had been told it was worth money, but he hadn't known how to sell it. Was it really worth anything?

Saad and Harding assured her it was valuable. They could hardly restrain their excitement as they went with her in search of Jabra. They found him in a coffee shop.

At first he wanted nothing to do with them, but when they said they were willing to pay him for what he had, his mood changed and he went willingly along to the Museum, where they showed him everything that had been gathered in their exploration of the cave. Suddenly he picked up a small object. It was his own cigarette roller! He could not afford ready-made cigarettes, and this roller was precious to him. He had lost it in the cave.

Here was further proof that the cave Captain Lippens, Brigadier Ashton and Captain Akkash had found was *the* cave.

Harding and Saad proceeded to question Jabra. Had his expedition found any entire scrolls? His reply was negative. They had only found big scraps such as the one he had at home. The big scrolls had already been taken out and sold to—

He stopped talking, realizing the discussion was leading him to a betrayal of the merchant and the Bedouins. Obviously terrified, he refused to say anything more.

Harding and Saad were relentless. They could not permit this vital information to slip through their fingers. They alternated threats of government punishment with strong assurances that Jabra was in absolutely no danger, if he told them the truth. They offered him money.

Finally the promise of money counterbalanced his fears and he mentioned Kando's name. He revealed that Kando and the Bedouins had more scraps of scrolls but were holding on to them for higher prices. The Jordan radio had carried news of the Metropolitan's reception in America, and had quoted a million dollars as the price he had placed on the scrolls.

The mystery was beginning to unravel. There was now a name and a man and a shop in Bethlehem to investigate.

War had disrupted regular transportation, so the next morning Saad, accompanied by two armed Museum guards, rode a donkey south along a dirt track to Bethlehem.

CHAPTER V

WHEN SAAD REACHED BETHLEHEM, however, he decided to leave the guards behind. Where shops were crowded and one roof was a stepping-stone to another, rumors traveled fast. Long before Saad could reach the shop Kando might hear of armed men approaching, and flee. The curator hoped he would not be recognized, but was prepared to admit, if necessary, that although he was connected with the Museum, he was dealing secretly for a private buyer.

When he found Kando's shop he saw it was dark inside. At first there seemed to be no one in it; then he noticed two men standing in the rear. They scrutinized him carefully, obviously trying to guess why he was there. Saad had had to ask directions, and the word had sped ahead of him through street and bazaar.

There was danger in this room for the curator. Kando, who knew he had broken the law, must fear imprisonment, and the loss of his shop and livelihood. He might resort to anything to prevent arrest. At the very least, what scraps of scrolls remained might be destroyed or hidden until they could be smuggled out of the country.

Before Saad could speak the older of the two men had reached him, pushed him back against the wall and held him pinned there. "Spy! Government spy!" he hissed. Standing between Saad and the doorway, he directed a stream of abuse at him.

The other man slid like an eel out of the door. Saad, while insisting he was not a spy, realized that the whole scene was being staged just to give the other a chance to get away. He must have been Kando, because as soon as he was gone the older man calmed down, mumbled to himself and took his hands off Saad.

It was clear now that Saad was an object of fear and suspicion. The sensible thing would have been to go back to Jerusalem, but Saad was both angry and determined. He sent the Museum guards home, and took a room for himself in Bethlehem. He had decided to stay until he could make Kando talk.

Each day he went to the shop, strolling in as if nothing important were on his mind. He examined the shop's wares, gossiped with the old man about the weather, the war, about anything but scrolls. And although he was afraid, he didn't show it. The shop was known to have connections with smugglers, and Saad was aware that he was under the surveillance of unsavory characters.

At first Kando would disappear as soon as Saad walked in. But gradually Kando began to stay longer, although he kept in the background. He was obviously puzzled. Saad wasn't behaving like a government official: making demands or giving orders. Kando began to listen, and now and then even joined in the conversation.

One day a boy was sent out for a tray of coffee. In Jordan one does not drink coffee with an enemy. Saad had won a victory. Kando was ready to hear what he had to say. Over the coffee the young curator broached the subject of the scrolls. He gave firm promises that no harm would come to Kando. He said that there was an English professor who wanted to buy whatever pieces of scrolls were left, and the transaction would be kept secret.

Kando relaxed. Yes, he had something to sell, but it must be handled in his own way. Saad was to go back to Jerusalem and wait; he would be contacted.

Kando visited Saad at the Museum, and the curator made a return visit to Bethlehem. These were evidently precautionary moves on the part of Kando, because no scroll fragments appeared. Saad had almost despaired when, several weeks later, Kando arrived at the Museum, requested that the curator see him in the garden where they could not be overheard, and showed him a large, dirty leather fragment.

Saad controlled his excitement. The writing on this fragment resembled the script he had seen on the tiny pieces scraped from the cave's floor. Yes, he assured Kando, he thought he had a buyer for this and any other scroll fragments Kando had.

"Bring the English professor to—," and Kando named the rendezvous, a hotel in Jericho.

Kando

Saad agreed. Of course, there was no English professor. A friend of Harding's, Mr. Richmond Brown, had agreed to play the part of a man who wanted the scroll fragments for his own private collection. Harding gave him one thousand pounds, about two thousand eight hundred dollars, but asked Brown to try to get the fragments for eight hundred pounds, if he could.

On the day of the rendezvous Saad and Brown made their way through narrow streets into a notoriously bad section of Jericho. They were genuinely fearful when they saw men lounging in doorways, watching their approach. A thousand pounds was a fortune to any of these men. Their fears were intensified when they came to the small, dirty hotel.

The proprietor motioned them into a side room where Kando and George Shaya were waiting. Kando stood near an open window. If an arrest was to be made when the money changed hands, he was prepared for escape; his men were stationed all around the outside of the hotel to protect him. No coffee was ordered. No pleasant formalities were exchanged. Saad asked if the fragments were there. Kando nodded, and then made a gesture of inquiry about the money.

It was expected of Saad to bargain. Instead, he took a chance, hoping to impress Kando.

"I came as a gentleman," he said. Then he stepped forward and placed the entire thousand pounds on the table. "If you, too, are a gentleman, you will show me what you have."

Kando *was* impressed. He would match Saad in dignity. He also stepped forward and put a small pile of fragments on the table.

The curator relaxed. All had gone amazingly well.

But then Brown, who had been tense throughout the interview, became stubborn. He felt obligated to try to get the fragments for less. He spoke up and said he would pay no more than eight hundred pounds.

Saad's heart sank. Kando would never settle for eight hundred, now that he had seen the thousand. And what would happen to the impression Saad had created, of gentlemen dealing with gentlemen, above such trifles as arguments over money? He had lost his advantage.

Kando was indeed annoyed. He gathered up the fragments. The atmosphere in the room turned cold and unfriendly. Since Brown was allegedly the buyer, there was nothing Saad could do but pick up the money and hope they could get away alive. Kando let them go, but on the long walk back to the Winter Palace Hotel, where Harding was staying, they were followed. In any one of these twisted streets they might be robbed and murdered. It was not an uncommon occurrence.

"If I'm going to be killed, I'll be killed," Saad thought fatalistically. "There's nothing I can do about it."

In all probability Kando had ordered that they not be molested, since they reached the Winter Palace Hotel safely. There they gloomily reported the unfortunate mistake, but Harding felt sure Kando would weaken and come to the Palestine Museum for the eight hundred pounds.

The next morning, after they had returned to Jerusalem, Kando did arrive at the Museum, but his manner had changed. He smiled, talked openly and boldly of the scrolls, and would not even consider eight hundred pounds. It was a thousand or nothing. Saad thankfully paid the sum and received the fragments.

Then Kando leaned forward and said: "Give my greetings to Mr. Harding."

He knew. His spies had seen Saad and Harding together the evening before, and Kando's nimble wits had told him that "the professor" was a blind, and that the real purchaser was the Jordanian government, in the person of Harding. The government was aware of all he, Kando, had done. Far from punishing him, Harding needed him. Kando was safe. He could now act as if any scroll transaction was a legitimate business deal.

Both Saad and Kando relaxed, and Saad could now ask who the Bedouins were. Did they have more fragments? Kando couldn't be sure, but he thought it possible. He also thought the Bedouins, having made money from one scroll cave, would be searching for others. But Kando would not go so far as to introduce Saad to them.

The curator dressed himself in an Arab burnoose and went to Bethlehem. He found the Taʻamireh there, but when he spoke to any of them they would not listen, brushing by him in the streets or crossing to avoid him.

One evening he saw that a group of about thirty Taʻamireh were making ready to leave their camp. They headed west, toward the desert. Recklessly, he decided to join them. If he could stay with them for a length of time, surely he'd find a chance to make friends.

Because it was dusk, at first they seemed not to know that a stranger was among them. Saad felt this was no ordinary pasturage trip. There were no women or children in the party. Gradually, he saw they had become aware of him and were uneasy. His attempts to address them were met with silence. Their pace increased until he could only keep up with them, with no breath to talk.

When it became dark, they stopped, made a fire and ate. He had no idea how far into the mountain pass they had gone. They isolated him, offering him neither food nor water. Suddenly a signal was given. The fire was extinguished. The tribesmen started out, but reversed their steps back to Bethlehem.

For Saad, it was a weird experience. They treated him as if he did not exist. And now he was in difficulty. He was hungry, thirsty, and in no physical condition for this double journey in one night.

As he plodded along it occurred to him that this was their way of getting rid of an unwelcome guest. They were afraid of him; they knew who he was; yet they did not dare touch him. But if he could not keep up with them and was left behind to wander or die, it would be no concern of theirs. He must keep up with them.

By the time Bethlehem came into view, before dawn, he was hobbling on sore feet, faint with hunger and exhaustion. When the others stopped at the camp he sat on the ground, too tired to go on into town.

Abruptly, everything seemed changed. He was offered food and drink. He was invited to rest on blankets by the fire. They not only spoke to him, but smiled, and he realized that he had passed a grueling test and had won their respect. The Bedouins set a high value on courage. They saw he was a man like themselves.

He told them, frankly, that he was acting for the Jordanian Department of Antiquities, but that Harding only wanted to talk to them about the scrolls, not to punish them. They had nothing to fear.

They believed Saad. Soon after they came to Amman to meet Harding, and told him the whole story of the discovery. They were at ease with him when they found he could speak their Ta'amireh dialect and understood their ways.

Harding was anxious that they continue looking for other cave depositories. Their desert and mountain skills were invaluable for such searches. But he tried to impress upon them that they must not disturb a cave, should they again find one that contained scrolls or jars or scroll parts.

They must leave it untouched, inform him of the discovery, let him examine the cave, and he would pay them for its contents. He explained how easily such old things were damaged by rough handling.

On this point Harding knew he had not succeeded. They became secretive, looking at each other but not at him. He could almost read their minds. Should they find any scrolls they would unquestionably take them, because only then could they be assured of bargaining power. It might be wrong to disturb a cave, but how else could they know what they had to sell?

He did not press the point. He might lose whatever trust they now had in him.

It was the spring of 1949. The war raged on. Although the archaeologists in Jordan knew that the Metropolitan in America had placed a sale value of a million dollars on his four scrolls, they did not know that Mar Athanasius' sale prospects were dubious. Many American institutions had seemed interested, and he had particularly hoped Yale University would be the purchaser. But, on February 25 of that year, an anonymous letter with only a New York address on it had been mailed to prospective purchasers, saying that the scrolls had been removed illegally from Jordan. In April both the Kingdom of Jordan and Israel laid claim to legal ownership of the scrolls. Doubt was cast on the Metropolitan's right to sell them, and would-be buyers were scared off.

In June a truce was declared between Israel and the Arab states, but any hopes of free communication between the archaeologists in Jordan and those of the Hebrew

University were dashed. There was still hostility. Barricades created a strip of no man's land between a divided Jerusalem. The Old City and some newer sections north, south and east outside its walls were part of Jordan; the western part of Jerusalem and west Palestine was Israeli. There was no mail or telephone service between the two countries.

The Palestine Museum, the monastery of St. Mark's, the American School of Oriental Research, and the French Dominican Bible and Archaeological School were in Jordan, while Hebrew University was in Israel.

However, communications between Jordan and the rest of the world resumed their normal course. In this way Harding and de Vaux learned there were scrolls of Isaiah both in America and in Israel, and that the other scrolls were of a religious nature but not books of the Old Testament. Scientific journals published excerpts from the Commentary of Habakkuk and mentioned another scroll which Dr. Burrows had named the Manual of Discipline, and which he had read through before leaving Jerusalem.

For a trained scholar in languages and paleography, accustomed to archaic scripts, none of the scrolls was difficult to read. It was not the first, quick reading but the detailed study, the interpretation, the relating of the scroll's contents to historical periods and events, the discussions of them with other scholars, that would take time.

The Isaiah scrolls were the simplest to study because the scholars were already familiar with Isaiah texts. Dr.

Burrows collated the entire text of the Metropolitan's scroll with the Masoretic text on board the ship taking him from Jerusalem to America. Dr. Sukenik's Isaiah was read just as quickly. One of the main results of their work established the fact that these scrolls agreed with the Masoretic text, except for some differences in spelling and grammar, rather than with the Septuagint.

Though this was of great interest to scholars, it did not necessarily prove that the Masoretic text was closer to the original Isaiah then the Septuagint. It might be that more than one version of the text had been in use two thousand years ago, one Jewish sect using one, and other Jews, a different one.

The other scrolls would require a great deal of study. Decomposition resulting in the blurring of words and lines was a serious problem, since the scholars could only guess at the obliterated parts. In addition to the actual meaning of the words, the religious, or historical role of the scrolls in the life of ancient Jews had to be evaluated. In this way it might be possible to ascertain when, and for what purpose, they had been written.

While the study of the texts was going on, Harding and de Vaux worked with what they had in Jordan. Everything collected from the cave had been taken to the Palestine Museum, where Joseph Saad had cleared out a room for the archaeologists' use.

The scroll fragments would have to wait. It would be a difficult, full-time task for experts, fitting hundreds of tiny pieces together. Instead, the two archaeologists began with the pottery shards.

These jars, similar to the ones reconstructed by Harding and de Vaux, are the only whole ones found.

They had only a description of the jars from the Bedouins, for Dr. Sukenik had not yet published his photographs. Spread out on a big table in the museum were large and small fragments out of which they must recreate a jar.

Day after day they worked, by trial and error. Sometimes it seemed hopeless.

"It's like having an automobile smashed to pieces in front of you," Father de Vaux grumbled, "and you have to put it together again without ever having seen the car when it was whole, or even a picture of it. And not just a car that will run, but it must look exactly like the original!"

95

It was an almost insurmountable task, but they succeeded. If two shards matched but curved in opposite ways, then they belonged on opposite sides. If a pottery piece was rounded at one end, the rounded part was either for top or bottom. So they worked for a month until they had reconstructed a complete jar.

True, the pieces did not fit perfectly, but when the spaces were filled in with plaster, they had a jar that stood upright, with a bowl-like lid fitting snugly over the neck. They looked at it with pride. It was the best they could do until they could see a picture of Dr. Sukenik's jars.

But such questions as: Who had put the jars in the cave? Who had written the scrolls? remained unanswered. And definite proof was still needed to set the period in which the scrolls had been created. Some scholars still scoffed at the idea that they were older than a century or two.

Harding and de Vaux returned to the area of the cave. In the heat of summer, wearing helmets to protect themselves against sunstroke, they trudged up the steep slopes until they reached the top of the flat plateau. They stood looking down at the desert and the blue Dead Sea. This strange phenomenon of nature is a large lake, not a sea, and although fed by the fresh waters of the Jordan, it is so salty a swimmer cannot sink in it. It is the lowest lake in the world, over twelve hundred feet below sea level.

As they stood with their backs to the mountain, the cave was behind them and farther up to their left on the mountain face. To their right was the long descent and walk to the spring of Ain Feshka. As far as they knew this area had always been the haunt of desert nomads seeking pasture for goats, or of bandits or exiles fleeing justice or injustice. In ancient Roman times there had been a military outpost here, but it was not the site for a town or village.

Yet the scribes of the scrolls must have lived somewhere nearby.

The archaeologists' first thought was of Ain Feshka, the small, beautiful pool of fresh water south of the plateau. It was fed by a mountain spring, and around it grew a narrow circle of vegetation. It was an attractive oasis, and must have been so in olden times.

They went down and studied it, but their trained eyes rejected it as a possibility. There was not the slightest evidence that people had ever lived there for any length of time. A settlement would have left some mark, even if soil had collected over it—a wall, a ditch, a burial mound. Ain Feshka was as flat as the rest of the wasteland that stretched from it to the Dead Sea.

There was only one other possibility. They discussed it, dismissed it, reconsidered it again and again, until at last it seemed to be the only one.

They returned to the top of the plateau. Here, at least, there *was* a ruin.

The plateau was called Qumran. A ruin, in Arabic, is *khirbet,* and so these particular low mounds and depressions of man-made stonework, almost obliterated by sand and marl, were known as Khirbet Qumran, the ruin of, or on, Qumran. Archaeologists like Harding and de Vaux had long known of it; in an earlier century explorers had thought it might be the ancient site of wicked Gomorrah. Modern archaeologists accepted it as the remains of an old Roman outpost. Jordan had many such old forts, and no attention had been paid to this one.

But now Harding and de Vaux examined it with fresh eyes. The nearly buried walls formed a rectangle about thirty yards by forty yards, just large enough to have housed a few soldiers. There was also a cistern, with steps leading down to it, that had probably once held water.

A short distance from the ruin was a graveyard. This was more interesting because it seemed, upon close observation, to be very large. A thousand graves didn't match up with an outpost for a few soldiers.

There was no harm investigating. They dug into several of the graves, and when they had unearthed the skeletons they looked at each other in amazement. This was a very strange graveyard indeed.

From their experience with other such burial places they knew this was neither Roman nor Arabic. If it had been Arabic the heads and feet of the dead would have been placed east to west as the Moslem religion required, not north to south as these were. It wasn't an ordinary ancient Jewish graveyard, either. There were no items of jewelry or personal ornaments such as were always found in old Jewish burial mounds. And, as the archaeologists investigated further, they found that almost all the skeletons were of men.

A thousand graves, and scarcely any in which women were buried? This was indeed a mystery. If an unknown people had been buried here, they must have lived in the area. Harding and de Vaux decided to dig into the old fort ruins and see what they could find.

In Jerusalem they collected the tools they would need and rounded up a few trusted workmen. When they drove back again the car was loaded down with tents and cooking equipment, and the paraphernalia of excavation: measuring tapes, T squares, notebooks, nails, levels, plumb bobs, picks, shovels, scoops, trowels, knives, planks, crowbars, hammers, and containers in which to carry away the excavated earth.

In addition, there were the chemical aids for cleaning metal objects. And packed away neatly were other small but necessary items: soft brushes, wire brushes, sandpaper, small tag labels, glass bottles, test tubes, pans and soap.

When everything had been transported to the plateau they stood for a moment looking at the ruin. The sun beat down on them, parching their mouths and burning exposed skin. Father de Vaux studied the scene that lay before them. "Archaeology," he remarked, "is a bore."

The remark was facetious. The Frenchman was devoted to his profession. But there was some truth in it; an archaeological dig like this one could mean weeks or months of patient excavation, only to find nothing of interest in the end.

Not for one moment could the workmen be left alone. A careless spade thrust might destroy something valuable.

The archaeologists watched carefully as the first pick loosened the soil, as the first spade went in close to the buried remains of a wall. Once the soil was loosened Harding and de Vaux sifted and sorted and examined, hoping to find man-made objects of metal or pottery.

They had worked for a few weeks, without success, when they had a brilliant idea.

Although a truce had been signed, both Jordanian and Israeli planes still flew overhead on reconnaisance missions, to photograph the boundary and see that neither side encroached on it. The planes gave them the idea, and Harding requested the Jordanian government to fly a plane over Khirbet Qumran and photograph it from the air.

When the photographic plates were developed and brought to the site the two men could hardly believe their eyes.

Faint, but unmistakable, lines and markings showed themselves underneath the topsoil; lines which extended far beyond the small rectangle of the Roman fort. These markings could never have been seen at ground level, but from the air they stood out. There had been something more here than just an outpost.

They renewed their digging with real fervor, using the new markings as their guidelines. Slowly the top of one wall was uncovered. It was not intact. Stones had been pushed off by drifting sand, but it extended beyond the fort.

Excavation continued as well within the boundaries of what had been the Roman fort itself, and there they

Aerial view of Qumran after excavation

made their first discovery, of coins. This was not surprising. Other objects might decompose, but metal lasts. The coins were gently separated from the gravelly, sandy soil in which they were embedded, treated with chemicals and washed. Then they could be deciphered. There were Roman coins of around A.D. 67 to 68; others from A.D. 69 to 73; still others ranging from A.D. 86 to 135.

But what of the faint tracery of walls seen in the aerial photographs, which extended beyond the fort? In the intense summer heat the archaeologists labored on. Harding's endless patience and de Vaux's vivid sense of humor kept the Arab workmen in good spirits. The only respite from the arduous labor were the trips made to Jerusalem for supplies or to catch up on their routine archaeological work which had been interrupted by the scroll discoveries.

As the weeks went by excitement gripped the camp at Qumran. The faint markings revealed by the photographs became the tops of extensive walls, showing that some large building had once stood there. It was not a village, bisected by streets or alleys. It seemed to be a compound, in which one room led directly into another, and the many rooms were bounded by a rambling outer wall.

At this period of excavation the outlines were neither sharp nor clear, but the archaeologists could see the pattern emerging. Now they made another discovery.

They had reached below the surface soil to a layer of a black substance. The two men rubbed the black stuff between their fingers, smelled it, and tested it in their field laboratory. It was the charred remains of reeds and palm wood, burned in a fire, and probably once used as roofing. Even in modern Jordan the tops of palm trees for roof poles and reeds for thatching were still used.

The fire had not been accidental. Not all the palm tree poles had burned, but the unburned ones had been deliberately trampled and destroyed when the fire was out. And, sifting through the ashes, the archaeologists found evidence of a battle. Arrowheads were scattered throughout the black stuff.

The coins and the fire were important historical clues. Roman coins were in circulation in Judaea, and Jews as well as Romans might have left them on Qumran, but it seemed more likely that since the smaller, more exposed part of the ruin had been a Roman military outpost the coins had been left there by Roman soldiers.

When and why had the military outpost been set up in the Wilderness, on the site of a former settlement building that had been the scene of a battle and set on fire? The dates on the coins and the archaeologists' knowledge of Jewish history helped them to guess the probable time. The earliest Roman coins found in the fort were dated A.D. 67 to 68, and it was in A.D. 68 that the Roman general Vespasian led his legions southward through the Jordan valley, burning and laying waste villages and settlements. This was the time of the First Jewish Revolt. The Second Jewish Revolt occurred in 132–135 and the more recent coins found in the fort dated from A.D. 86 to 135.

This was more than just coincidence, and the archaeologists felt certain the military outpost had been built at the time of the first revolt and was still in use during the second. And it was known, from Josephus' *Antiquities of the Jews*, that Vespasian had visited the Dead Sea in the month of June, A.D. 68, after attacking Jericho; if there had been a Jewish settlement there he would certainly have marched on it and taken it, killing the inhabitants and setting fire to whatever would burn.

In this way the archaeologists began to reconstruct the events of the distant past. Now it seemed as if certain conjectures could be assumed as true: that there had been a settlement of Jews on Qumran, that they had been destroyed by Vespasian, and that Roman soldiers had then used part of the building as a small fort. The plateau would be excellent, from a military standpoint, since it dominated the surrounding area—especially the caves in the mountain which might otherwise have given refuge to Jewish rebels.

The choice of Qumran for a settlement, or large dwelling place, was still a puzzle. It was conceivable that active rebels might throw up hasty fortifications against an expected siege during the revolts, but the tops of the uncovered walls showed a thick, sturdy masonry, which had not been built in haste.

But if the inhabitants had been peaceful men, why had they chosen Qumran? Ancient Jews were farmers, living near their vineyards or orchards, or they were fishermen or nomadic shepherds, or town or village dwellers. They would not normally pick such a place as this plateau, where the soil was barren and the only fresh water nearby was the small pool of Ain Feshka.

CHAPTER VI

Harding and de vaux had dug up the first grave in the summer of 1949. The winter had passed in the slow toil of excavation; it was the spring of 1950. Both felt the pressure of other responsibilities, either in Amman or at the Palestine Museum or the Dominican School in Jerusalem, but still they continued to spend as many days and nights on the plateau as they could.

They read the scientific journals with great interest, watching for the publication of scroll texts, or for articles about them. The scholars of the world, in turn, followed with fascination the work at Qumran and the news of the buried building, the coins, the evidences of a deliberate fire, and the archaeologists' reconstruction of Vespasian's raid.

In Israel, Dr. Sukenik, his son Yigael Yadin, and other scholars had published excerpts from the scroll of hymns, which had so startled Dr. Sukenik when he had first seen it three years before. He named it *Hodayot*, the Hebrew for "Thanksgiving Psalms." Written in the style of the Psalms, it was an original and beautiful work.

In the text the writer described himself as a man who had many enemies, *but who also had many followers who flocked to him.* He was persecuted by one man in particular, the scroll stated, "For he has driven me from my country like a bird from its nest."

From this it was reasonable to guess that the author had been a religious leader, in opposition to powerful people, but who had been surrounded by followers who believed as he did.

In March of 1950 parts of another scroll in the possession of the Hebrew University were ready for publication. The scroll was called "The War of the Sons of Light Against the Sons of Darkness." It was another original work, not part of the Bible, and a very strange document.

It divided the people of Judaea into the Sons of Light, who kept a special covenant with God, and the Sons of Darkness. It predicted the coming of a great war between these two forces, which was to last exactly forty years. The Messiah would then appear and insure victory for the faithful Sons of Light. They would be helped by angels who would fight on their side.

The prophecy announced when the war would start and that the fighting would commence with a great roll of trumpets. It even portrayed a final victory. It catalogued in detail how the soldiers were to be recruited, how the armies and battalions were to be organized. It listed the weapons to be used and the battle tactics for each

A scroll fragment of "The War of the Sons of Light Against the Sons of Darkness" single year. It also presented an elaborate description of a signals system, and of the priestly benedictions, and the banners and ceremonies to be used and the prayers to be said on specific days of the battle.

The scroll was strange because it described in detail a battle that was yet to take place. Even odder was the fact that it revealed a religious faith in many ways unlike the prevailing Jewish religion of two thousand years ago—a belief in angels, and a separate covenant made with God, a covenant based on the Law of Moses but which excluded those Jews who were Sons of Darkness.

The scroll specifically named all who fell into the category of Sons of Darkness, against whom the great war was to be launched. They were the troops of Edom, Moab, Ammon, the Philistines, the Kittim of Asshur, and the Offenders of the Covenant.

Modern scholars knew that the Edomites, Moabites, Ammonites and Philistines were traditional enemies of ancient Judaea. The Offenders of the Covenant, on the other hand, were Jews who refused to believe as did the Sons of Light. Scholars had known there were political-religious divisions in Judaea two thousand years ago under the Romans, but not that there had been such strong enmity.

And who were the Kittim? The editors and other scientific interpreters agreed it was a code word, but for what enemy? Some thought that Kittim referred to either the Greek or Greek-Seleucid conquerors of Judaea, and that the scroll was referring to an age gone by. Many other scholars, including Dr. Burrows, Professor Yadin, and Father de Vaux, felt the Kittim were the Roman tyrants of the last century B.C. and the first century A.D.

Thus the scroll, while it presented a wealth of new information, also raised new questions. The historians could not fit its contents into what they knew of Judaea. It would have helped if they could have been absolutely certain of when the scrolls had been written, but to many this still remained a controversial issue.

In November of 1950 Professor Solomon Zeitlin wrote an article for the *Jewish Quarterly Review,* an American publication, in which he still claimed that the scrolls were either complete forgeries or else were works of the Middle Ages.

But that same month, the famous carbon 14 test of the linen wrappings of the scrolls was made at Chicago University by Professor W. F. Libby.

All living organisms breathe carbon dioxide. In addition to the normal, stable carbon with an atomic weight of 12, all living plants and animals absorb a radioactive carbon from the earth's upper atmosphere—carbon 14. Professor Libby had been awarded a Nobel prize for his process of dating by carbon 14. He had experimented and proved that after a living organism dies, the radioactivity created by this carbon remains in the dead plant or animal but disintegrates at a constant rate. In the first 5,500 years it loses half its life; the loss of two-thirds or three-fourths can thus also be accurately measured. It is therefore possible to calculate the age of ancient organic matter from the amount of carbon 14 remaining in it.

The linen wrappings of the scrolls, made from the flax

plant, were used in the test. A sample was burned and then measured for carbon radioactivity with a very sensitive radiation meter. Allowing for a two-hundred-year possible margin of error, the test placed the cutting of the flax between 168 B.C. and A.D. 233, and Professor Libby's closest calculated date was A.D. 33.

The test was enormously important. It confirmed the

A bit of the linen wrapping that protected one of the scrolls found in Cave One

belief of those scholars who had said the scrolls were two thousand years old. It also gave Harding and de Vaux new confidence that their archaeological work at Qumran had a relation, in age, to the scrolls.

The excavations were bringing to light the existence not only of outer walls but of inner ones—some small enough to have confined rooms, and some large enough for courtyards. In the northwest corner the walls were higher than elsewhere, forming a two-storied building that was unquestionably a watchtower. Such towers had been common in ancient villages and large dwellings.

At night, while the hyenas seemed to mock everything human with their hideous cries, the two archaeologists built their campfire and sat close to it, talking. Sometimes Joseph Saad or Dr. Awni Dajani, Harding's assistant in the Antiquities ℸepartment, joined them.

They could now be reasonably certain that the scrolls had been written in the first century A.D., or in the last century B.C. They could be just as certain that a large settlement of Jews had lived on the Qumran plateau at that time and had been driven out or destroyed by Vespasian in A.D. 68. They could assume a connection between the scrolls and the settlement.

But the contents of the scrolls only deepened some of the mysteries. Were the inhabitants of Qumran the Sons of Light? Was this a place of exile for persecuted people? Was it here they had made a special covenant with God, and projected their vision of a great, victorious war to come?

There had been political-religious differences among

the Jews of the first century, principally between the parties of the Pharisees, the Sadducees and the Zealots. To understand these differences it is necessary to review Jewish history back to the second century B.C., the age of Antiochus IV, 175–164 B.C.

Judaea was then a conquered country, and Antiochus was its Greek tyrant. He had imposed heavy taxes and tried to force Greek laws and gods upon the Jews. They had resisted, defying tax collectors and refusing to worship any god but their own.

In 168 B.C., the father and sons of the Hasmonean family led a revolt. They went to the hills and called upon all Judaea to rise and fight Antiochus. An army was gathered, and after years of fierce battles the Jewish revolt was successful, and Antiochus' reign came to an end in 164.

Judaea was independent. Only one of the Hasmoneans survived the war; he was now proclaimed high priest, commander of the army, and a prince. In actual fact his descendants, called the Hasmonean dynasty, became kings. Perhaps such strong rulers were necessary, since Judaea was surrounded by powerful enemies. But many Jews were offended. A Jewish tyrant was not much better than a foreign one. Besides, the Hasmoneans had no religious right to offer the sacrifice in the Temple of Jerusalem. They were not of the ancient order of High Priests and they had usurped this sacred authority.

The population began to split into parties. Some upheld Hasmonean rule, others questioned it or were disobedient. Tension slackened or tightened, depending upon the nature of the Hasmonean king.

One of them, Alexander Jannaeus, 103–76 B.C., was so horribly cruel, and his efforts to crush any opposition so harsh, that he served only to intensify the divisions among the Jews. He stirred the people to wrath and disgust. If Jews got in the way of his ambitions he killed them as quickly as he would foreigners.

Civil war broke out. Alexander Jannaeus eventually suppressed it, and when it was over he held a victory banquet at his palace in Jerusalem. He feasted where he could look out upon a field on which eight hundred prisoners, his own people, were being crucified. The wives and children of his victims were forced to stand there and watch them die.

The Hasmonean dynasty continued, even though the rulers became puppet kings when Rome conquered Judaea and made it a province. The most pious Jews blamed the Hasmoneans for their troubles, equally with the Romans. They believed God was angry because the Hasmoneans had usurped the rights of the High Priests of the Temple. Factions evolved among the Jews. They were the Pharisees, the Sadducees and the Zealots.

The Pharisees were not active rebels. Their resistance took the form of a scrupulous observance of the Law of Moses and of the traditional laws that had grown up over the centuries. They were fond of arguing over small points of conduct, dietary rules and special Sabbath laws, and were nicknamed "the lawyers." Their opponents called them hypocrites, saying they substituted ritual formalities for a true dedication to holiness.

The Sadducees were the party of the wealthy Jews, the nobility and priests. They also claimed to uphold the

Law of Moses, but they adopted many foreign ideas from the Greeks and Romans.

The Zealots were a smaller party, fiery men of action, who eventually led the disastrous revolts against the Romans in the first century A.D. Their enmity was principally against the foreign conquerors.

The ideas set forth in the scrolls did not seem to fit any of these groups. Sadducees, Pharisees and Zealots continued to offer their sacrifices in the Temple in Jerusalem; they were not in exile; they had not made a *new* covenant with God, but considered themselves upholders of the Mosaic covenant. The Zealots were not waiting for a Messiah to lead them into revolt.

In December of 1950 the Habakkuk Commentary and the Isaiah scroll were published in their entirety in America. The Commentary was of particular interest to all the archaeologists who were endeavoring to find a relationship between the scrolls and the historical period in which they were written.

It, like the scroll of the Sons of Light Against the Sons of Darkness, spoke of the Kittim, designating them as the enemy coming from across the sea to subjugate every nation. And, like the Thanksgiving Hymns, it spoke of a persecuted leader, but far more explicitly. He was the Teacher of Righteousness, the leader of a sect who were the "doers of the Law" or the "men of Truth." Opposed to him was the Wicked Priest who persecuted both the Teacher and his followers. The Lord, stated the Commentary, would take vengeance against the Kittim, against the Wicked Priest, and against all those who had not supported the Teacher.

Excerpts from the Habakkuk Commentary had been released before and had given rise to much scholarly speculation, but when the whole was published the questions it raised were discussed not only by scholars but received widespread coverage by newspaper and magazine writers. Wild guesses were made. A few thought that Jesus was the Teacher of Righteousness, and the High Priest of the Temple the wicked persecutor. Others argued that the Teacher was an unknown religious leader, but that the Wicked Priest could only be Alexander Jannaeus.

If the latter supposition were true, then the scroll's original author had written of a happening during Jannaeus' reign, 103–76 B.C.

Aside from these questions, the scroll gave definite proof of the existence of a sect, a special party among the Jews, who had lived together in exile, separated themselves from the rest of Judaea and refused to honor the Temple in Jerusalem.

The evidence focused more attention on Qumran. Here a complex of rooms was being uncovered, large enough to have sheltered a settlement of men—of men, because further explorations of the graves confirmed that very few of the thousand burials had been of women. Qumran could have been a sort of monastery, a place of voluntary exile for a persecuted leader and his followers.

There was an ancient Jewish sect that fitted the descriptions in the scrolls. Although Yigael Yadin believed his father had been the first to name the Essenes, Dr. Burrows had suggested the Essenes as a possibility to Trever and Brownlee while they were all three still in

Jerusalem. In the midst of wilder speculations among scholars, more and more of them were accepting this theory.

Who were the Essenes?

The first-century A.D. writer Flavius Josephus, in his *The Wars of the Jews*, had written: "For there are three philosophical sects among the Jews . . . the Pharisees . . . the Sadducees; and the third sect, who pretend to a severer discipline, are called Essenes."

And the historian Pliny wrote: ". . . on the west side of the Dead Sea . . . is the solitary tribe of the Essenes."

Pliny called them a tribe, but according to Josephus they were a religious-political party. He described two types of Essenes: those who remained in villages and towns, but kept themselves apart from their neighbors, following their own stern code, and the larger number who lived together in one community, in one place.

They were extremely pious, scorning worldly interests. They believed they, alone, upheld the Law of Moses. They also followed new rituals they had adopted to prove their special covenant with God.

New members had to pass a rigorous initiation period. Once they became a part of the community their days were passed in strict routine. Before sunrise they prayed, then they were sent out to work by their stewards, until the fifth hour. At that time they assembled together, purified themselves in water and put on white clothing. Their dining hall was a sacred place of meeting. After eating and praising God they changed their white garments for work clothes, and labored again until the evening meal, which was the same formal, holy affair.

Priests and overseers commanded obedience. The Essenes made their own laws, exacted their own punishments. No one had personal possessions or money; all was owned in common. If the people who lived at Qumran were Essenes, this would explain why no jewelry or money had been found in the graves.

Positive proof that the scroll authors were Essenes and that the Qumran settlement had been the Essenes' was not established, but both were certainly very likely possibilities. If the sect called themselves Sons of Light, it was also probable that the name Essenes was one given to them by outsiders, and was not one of the names they used to describe themselves.

It was now 1951, and in the spring of that year Dr. Burrows published the photographs and transcription of another scroll, which he called, "The Manual of Discipline."

Next to the Habakkuk Commentary, this was the most valuable of all the scrolls to historians and archaeologists, if not to Bible scholars. In plain language it set forth the theology, the laws, the discipline, the everyday life of a sect which had striking similarities to the Essene sect as described by Josephus. If it was granted that Josephus and the Manual of Discipline scroll were speaking of the same people, then the scroll was an authentic account of Essene life. Josephus had been an outsider. He wrote of what he heard, but the author of the Manual wrote of what he knew.

The sect seemed to use many different names for itself—the Congregation, the Community, the Men of the Covenant, the Sons of Light. Although marriage was not forbidden, life appeared to be chiefly male and monastic. Membership was not obtained by birth but by merit and proved dedication. Not until an applicant reached the age of twenty-five could he be appointed to his place in the community.

A new applicant was questioned closely as to why he had chosen voluntary exile; if his reasons were sincere he could stay, but only to learn the principles and rules of the sect.

After that first study period he was examined again, and his case presented to the Many, those who had attained full membership. Even if they approved him, he would be on probation for another year. During that time he must sell any property he had and give his money to the Overseer. He was assigned work to do and given clothes to wear and there was more ritual that he must learn.

At the end of that year he was either rejected finally or admitted into full association with the Many. He went through an initiation ceremony, partook of purification and of the sacred banquets presided over by the priests and elders.

But life was not simple, even then. Discipline was harsh. The usual punishment was a curtailment of the food ration, but for serious offenses a member might be reduced to the status of probationer or even cast out of the sect completely.

Some of the offenses and punishments were:

"A man who consciously lies in the matter of his wealth . . . is to be regarded as outside membership (for one year) and is to be fined of one fourth of his food ration."

"If a man answer his neighbor defiantly or speak brusquely so as to undermine the composure of his fellow, and in so doing flout the orders of one who is registered as his superior . . . he is to be fined for one year."

Other punishments were equally severe: for foolish speech, three months' banishment from the membership; for interrupting another person speaking, ten days; for sleeping during a session of the Many, thirty days; for leaving a session without permission, ten days; for foolish laughter, thirty days; for slandering his fellow member, banishment for one year; for slandering the faith of the community, banishment forever.

Every member was responsible to his immediate superior in rank. The entire community was reviewed each year, and members were moved up or down in rank, according to merit or lack of it.

Authority over the community was vested in three priests and twelve elders. Under them were officers who acted as Overseers of the different kinds of work. Four priests and six laymen were appointed judges. Whenever there were ten members working together or standing guard at night, a priest must be with them to chant the hymns. Members, too, chanted as they worked: their prayers stormed Heaven day and night.

There was a certain amount of democracy. In council session even the newest member had the right to speak, in turn. If it was an urgent matter a member could even rise out of turn and ask permission by stating: "I have something to say to the Community." If all agreed, he was given this extraordinary privilege.

The communal meal, or banquet, seemed to be a kind of substitute place of worship, since the sect refused to worship at the Temple in Jerusalem. At the meal the High Priest first blessed the bread, then in turn each member of the community did the same. There was evidence in the scroll that the sect rejected the Jerusalem Temple, not only because they felt the Temple was defiled by priests who had no right to offer up the sacrifice there, but because the sect made use of a different calendar.

When the fragments found by Harding and de Vaux were studied later, more information came to light. The sect had a calendar which was based on their own interpretation of the book of Genesis: a 364-day year, months of thirty days, and four additional days, one after each three-month period. This was contrary to the lunar calendar used by the rest of Judaea, so the Sabbaths and the high holy festivals of the year could not coincide. This alone would have been enough to divide the sect from the rest of the Jews, and the Manual of Discipline indicated they were persecuted as a result of it.

The Manual of Discipline was of great importance. The mystery of who had written the scrolls and why they should be found in the Wilderness had been partly solved by the Habakkuk Commentary, and now the Manual shed more light on the distant past. The Teacher of Righteousness and the Wicked Priest were still unknown figures, but it seemed definite that a leader, or a succession of them, had founded a community in exile, and that it had existed for a long time before the first century A.D.

Again the evidence made it seem likely the sect was Essene.

Controversy, as well as enlightenment, followed the publication of the Manual of Discipline. Books were written, newspaper and magazine articles printed, attempting to prove that Jesus must have been an Essene, and that the Essenes' communal meal was the forerunner of the supper and blessings of the early Christians.

The more cautious scholars refrained from jumping to such conclusions, seeing as many differences between Essenic and Christian beliefs as there were similarities. For example, the sect mentioned in the Manual and the Habakkuk Commentary did not expect one Messiah, but two. One was to be a warlike king, from the house of David, who would lead them into battle, and the other a spiritual leader, who was to come from the priestly house of Zadok.

It was hoped that additional light on the many questions would be shed as a result of the excavations going on at Qumran.

CHAPTER VII

THE WORK OF EXCAVATION was slow and arduous. Every spadeful of dislodged earth had to be sifted. There was always the chance that a small object like a coin, an earring, a broken fragment of a lamp, might be stuck to the underside of a stone, so discolored and misshapen the eye would not quickly distinguish it.

A larger crew of workmen was impractical, as they could never be properly supervised by only two archaeologists. The excavation could not be rushed, and sometimes bad weather stopped it for weeks at a time.

Yet Harding and de Vaux were making progress. In addition to the uncovering of horizontal layers, a deep vertical trench was made in one place.

This is a usual archaeological method, to observe the successive periods of occupation of a dwelling place and to search for man-made objects in the various strata.

They found coins on different levels. Near the surface

Father de Vaux (left) and Father Rouset discussing excavation plans

G. Lankester Harding (left), a visitor, and Father Joseph Milik examining one of the excavated rooms at Qumran

of the earth were some from the Roman Empire, but below there were others. Three silver coins came from the age of Antiochus VII, dated 136, 130 and 129 B.C. Thirty-eight coins were of the era of Alexander Jannaeus, 103–76 B.C., although not all of the Jannaeus coins were found in the trench cut; some were collected later from other sections of the building.

The two archaeologists were excited over the find, but too cautious definitely to date the building back to the time of Antiochus. Coins are a good indication in estimating a period, but they can be misleading because they have a long life and can stay in circulation fifty years or more after they are minted.

But certainly it would be established that Qumran had been a dwelling place in Alexander Jannaeus' day. If the people of Qumran were the Essenes of the scrolls, their exile might have taken place at that time, but not much earlier.

The theory that Alexander Jannaeus was the Wicked Priest gained more credence. But it was still only a possibility.

The excavations continued to turn up a coin here and there until a continuity from 136 B.C. to the Roman era became apparent—with one noticeable gap. There was only one coin found from the reign of King Herod, in the latter part of the last century B.C.

One day Harding and de Vaux completed the digging out of steps leading down to a cistern. Across those steps was a great, jagged crack; the lower stairs were not in

Earthquake crack in cistern stairs

124|

line with the upper ones. It was exactly the kind of crack that would have been made by an earthquake.

And there had been a terrible earthquake in King Herod's time, in 31 B.C. Records indicated the devastation it had caused and the number of people who had been killed.

Standing above, looking down at that great crack in the steps, the two men could well imagine the disaster of an earthquake on Qumran: walls shaking, rocks cascading down onto the plateau from the mountain, the shifting of the earth.

The inhabitants must have fled, and stayed away for the many years of Herod's reign. This explained the break in the continuity of the coins. Then they had returned and rebuilt the settlement and had remained there until the Roman legions had finally destroyed them.

One other important clue was revealed by the coins. In a dwelling place of this size, made to shelter an entire community and lived in for at least a century, there was a remarkable scarcity of money uncovered. From their experience in other diggings, Harding and de Vaux would have expected much more. However, if the dwellers had been Essenes this was understandable, since the Essenes despised money.

The two archaeologists could feel, looking across the jumble of upturned earth at the emerging walls, that they were making progress. Expectation grew every day. They were hopeful that evidence connecting Qumran to the scrolls lay buried here; any day, a spade might turn up the necessary link or proof. They worked even longer hours than before. But their work was to be interrupted.

Joseph Saad was sitting at his desk in the Palestine Museum one July afternoon in 1951. Though it was hot outside, the room was pleasantly cool and he could concentrate on his papers. Suddenly, though he had heard no sound, he knew he was not alone. He looked up.

In the doorway were several Bedouins, silently waiting. They were pleased at his welcome, and came in. A Bedouin held out leather fragments, one of which was as large as the palm of Saad's hand.

"Where did you find it?" he asked.

In a new cave, they answered, far to the south of Qumran. They would not tell him where, and only when they found it was Harding who would pay for the fragments would they agree to wait for him.

A messenger was sent to Qumran, and Harding came as quickly as his old car would bring him. He paid the Bedouins the price agreed upon: one English pound, about $2.80, for each square inch. But when he questioned them about the new cave they gave evasive answers. All he learned was that they had seen no jars or complete scrolls.

Harding felt it was useless to try to locate the cave himself. *South* could mean anywhere from five to twenty-five miles below Qumran. He could only urge the Bedouins to discuss the matter among themselves, to trust him to pay them for taking him to see the cave and for anything they found there. He asked them to return when their decision was made.

He emphasized his trust in them, knowing they would

appreciate it. Yet it was difficult to go back to Qumran to wait for developments. Father de Vaux expressed his own frustration at the secrecy of the Bedouins, in explosive comments, but agreed Harding had done all he could.

Months went by. To add to their worries came rumors that pieces of leather fragments had found their way to various dealers' shops and were being offered for sale. Joseph Saad bought as many as he could find. They proved to be fragments of Biblical books that strictly followed the Masoretic text, and were judged to be of a later date than the scrolls of Qumran.

The archaeologists had almost given up in despair when finally the Ta'amireh Bedouin tribesmen consented to lead Harding and de Vaux to the new discoveries. There was not one cave, but four, and they were at Wady Murabba'at, about ten miles south of Qumran.

No one but Bedouins could have found them. The Wady Murabba'at was a deep canyon running east to west, starting close to Bethlehem, slicing through the Judaean mountains in a jagged, winding course. The canyon sides were nearly perpendicular, and eight hundred feet deep where they met the Dead Sea.

All four caves were on the north side, high on the precipice wall. The archaeologists had been warned of the difficulty in reaching them, so they had brought camping equipment. After a terrifying climb they reached the first cave. Night had fallen and they thought themselves lucky to find an eight-foot-wide ledge where they could pitch their tents.

They were standing in the mouth of the cave, shining their torches inside it, when a huge boulder crashed down the canyon side, flattening one of the tents as if it had been made of paper. Hastily they gathered up the remainder of the equipment, and spent the rest of the night crouched in the cave.

When morning came they realized why the Bedouins had agreed to bring them here. The cave was a frightful place; the Bedouins had explored as deeply as they dared go. There were great, yawning pitholes in the floor. The roof threatened to give way; sand and earth frequently slid down or rocks suddenly fell. The cave seemed to have no end, but wound on into utter blackness.

No scrolls were found, but there was evidence the cave had been used as a hideout by Zealot rebels in the Second Jewish Revolt. One leather fragment purchased from the Bedouins had been signed by Simon Ben Kosebah, or Bar Kosebah, the leader of the Second Revolt, traditionally known as Bar Chocheba.

When the fragment was photographed and published Yigael Yadin's reading of it was: "Simon ben Kosebah to Joshua ben Galgola and soldiers of the fortress, greetings. I take heaven to witness against me: mobilize from the Galileans whom I have saved (or whom you have saved) everyone, for I shall put irons on your feet as I did to ben Aphlul. Simon ben Kosebah, Prince of Israel."

Harding and de Vaux wished to explore all the Wady Murabba'at caves, but this first inspection convinced them a full-scale expedition must be organized, which would take time and preparation, and it could wait. They did not want to leave the work at Qumran just at this moment.

Also, at the Palestine Museum two expert scholars of the Dominican School were beginning the delicate, difficult task of assembling the tiny fragments found in the floor of the Qumran cave. A room was assigned to them, and all day Father J. T. Milik and Father D. Barthélemy bent over the fragments, sorting and piecing them together, transcribing what they found.

A fragment might contain one word or half a word. The other half might be somewhere among the pieces inside the glass slides: finding it was a maddening task.

In the room where they worked stood the jar which Harding and de Vaux had reconstructed. Dr. Sukenik had published photographs of the two jars he had bought, and it was astonishing how closely the one pieced together from imagination resembled the original.

And at Qumran the excavations were taking shape. To the inexperienced eye it might seem confusing, since the work had progressed unevenly. In places only a foot of the walls broke the surface, elsewhere the digging was almost down to floor level. Piles of discarded earth were everywhere.

The archaeologists, however, could see that there was one central rectangle about forty yards long and thirty yards wide, divided into rooms and courtyards inside. Branching off from this center were annexes of other rooms.

At this time Harding and de Vaux concentrated on the main rectangle, starting with the watchtower in the northwest corner. By November of 1951 they had cleared the base of the tower, almost forty feet square. In their opinion the first story, which was windowless, had been used as a storeroom, probably for weapons. A spiral staircase had led to the second story, which was divided into three rooms. From one room a door opened to what must have been a wooden gallery along the west wall. This was a guess, based on the fact that there was no outside gallery of stone, and a wooden one could have burned in the Roman fire.

The digging moved east of the tower. In the cold winter winds the archaeologists and their helpers were glad to be below plateau level, where the ancient walls gave some protection from the gritty sand that blew into their eyes.

They excavated a long room that was too narrow to have been anything but a storeroom. Then they started on a large one, next to it. Here they came upon the first find that indicated something about the way of life of the people of the settlement.

The room was a kind of huge pantry with over a thousand dishes, some broken, some intact. They were made of pottery. Although time and the shifting of sandy earth had disarranged their neatness, it was clear they had been left stacked bowl on bowl, platter on platter, and cup on cup.

They were an exciting discovery, the first tenuous link with the scrolls, since the Manual of Discipline described a community which ate together. The great quantity of dishes indicated a large number of inhabitants served by a common kitchen.

The kitchens adjoined the pantry. Their identity was

certain because there were fireplace hearths for cooking, and in one room a bake oven.

The digging progressed east and south of the watchtower. A courtyard had served the kitchen and pantry area, dividing it from the rooms where the archaeologists now began to dig.

From the top of the walls of one room, the archaeologists looked down at the earth that blocked it, and wondered for what this room could have been used. Its narrowness suggested a storeroom, but it was too far from the kitchen and service area.

For a week they toiled, with nothing to show for their efforts. Then, halfway down, the spades struck a large, hard object. While Harding and de Vaux worked with the smallest tools and even their hands to free it from the encrustation of soil and gravel, a workman's spade hit another one.

Finally they could lift out the two heavy objects, and found they were parts of a plaster structure with a brick base. Lying separately, they had no familar shape. It was impossible to guess what these objects were. They were wrapped in thick folds of tarpaulin and stowed in the car, to be taken to Jerusalem.

It was time, anyway, to break camp for a while. The weather looked stormy and the workmen were due for a rest.

Central pillar, which supported a spiral staircase. The staircase made it possible for those in the watchtower to communicate with the rooms in the lower part of the tower.

At the Palestine Museum, while Joseph Saad again arranged for a room where they could continue their work, Harding and de Vaux visited their colleagues. Watching Milik and Barthélemy bending over hundreds of scroll fragments, their noses practically touching them as they strained to make out the writing, their eyes bloodshot, the two archaeologists were grateful for the outdoor life of Qumran. The heat, the cold, the sandstorms, the backbreaking labor, even the occasional nuisance of a poisonous viper, were preferable to this nerve-racking job of transcription.

When their room was ready they placed the plaster objects on a table. It was an effort to lift them, even with Saad's help.

Now began that archaeological task which is pure artistry, the delicate re-creation of a broken structure into its original shape. The object must not be forced into a shape it never had, or driven into form by a hasty theory.

As with all successful creative work, there came a moment when suddenly everything fitted. The mortar they were using molded the pieces together in harmony. There had been a week of frustration; now the job was done. The two men looked at what they had wrought and could scarcely believe it.

Before them was proof that the scrolls in the cave came from the building on the plateau.

It was an ancient writing table used by scribes. Seventeen feet in length, it afforded space for scrolls to be stretched out and sewn together, square by square. It was low, only twenty inches off the ground, but scribes in Palestine sat cross-legged upon the ground or on a bench only a few inches high.

To add to the evidence, the next expedition to Qumran uncovered a desk top in the same room, with two hollows carved into its surface, and two inkwells. One was of brass, the other of clay; there was even a hard residue of carbon ink left in each of them.

Such moments as these made up for all the days and weeks and months of drudgery. Father de Vaux joked about the boredom of archaeology, but exulted over its rewards.

The ink residue, when tested, was found to be the same type of ink as used on the scrolls. The two hollows in the desk top might have been used to hold the inkwells, but most likely had served as containers for the purifying water in which the scribes dipped their fingers before writing holy script. The room was now identified as "the scriptorium," and its furnishings were completed by the discovery of several smaller tables and a low plaster bench which ran along the base of the walls.

Another discovery, later, underscored the evidence that the scribes of the Qumran settlement were, indeed, the creators of the scrolls. A jar was found, similar in design to those found in the cave.

The rooms adjoining the scriptorium presented the archaeologists with a confusing problem because the Romans, who had occupied them, had cleared them out, burned the debris and partitioned them into smaller cubicles. These later partitions had to be removed before the rooms' original boundaries could be seen.

Directly east was a large room, empty except for a circle of stones in the floor centered at one end of it. They had not been used as a hearth, since the stones were not scorched. What could they be? It was a puzzle until one day de Vaux, who happened by accident to be standing in the circle, addressed Harding at the other end of the room. They realized instantly that the circle of stones was a speaker's place.

This, then, had been the dining room and assembly hall of the inner group of those in full membership. Another large room nearby was probably the council chamber where everyone, including probationers, had gathered, while the dining hall was reserved for the affairs of the initiated.

An empty cistern was found close to the room with the stone circle. It increased the likelihood that this room had been the dining hall, since the diners would have gone through a water purification ceremony before eating.

The findings at Qumran were published in scholarly journals, and stirred tremendous interest. The work of transcription and the work of excavation had so complemented each other that it was as if the Essenes of Qumran had been brought back to life. Homely objects

Joseph Saad, at the reconstructed writing table found in the scriptorium, examines one of the ancient inkwells.

Reconstructed desk top. The hollows may have held the water needed by the scribes for the ritual hand-washing performed before starting work on a sacred text.

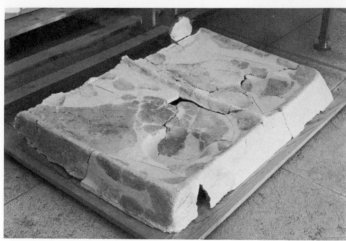

such as dishes, tables, bake ovens and writing desks were tangible evidence of what had been merely conjecture.

There was more excavating to be done at Qumran, but temporarily this work had to be interrupted because an expedition was organized at this time to investigate the caves at Wady Murabba'at. Harding and de Vaux led the expedition, which left on January 21, 1952.

The trails were so dangerous that even the mules balked, and all the supplies and equipment had to be

A section of the council chamber. The small, plastered recess was probably used for water storage.

carried by the archaeologists and their Bedouin crew. They relayed their backpacks from one resting place to another. Since they had already looked at Cave One, they started with the second of the four.

They had to clear the entrance of obstacles before they could walk in, upright. At first they enjoyed rolling out the huge boulders and letting them bounce and smash down the cliff, but they soon stopped when they realized the impacts were starting rock slides within the cave.

When the entrance was cleared, the Bedouins hung back. The depths of the cave were fearsome. The Bedouins never ventured farther than the mouth. Harding persuaded one of the Ta'amireh to go with him, to carry the paraffin flare. They had gone about fifty feet, burrowing through rock tunnels on their stomachs, blinded by dust and choked by the smoke from the flare, when the Ta'amireh who was ahead of Harding suddenly disappeared and the flare was extinguished.

In all his long career, Harding said afterward, he had never been so terrified. It was pitch-black. He could neither see nor hear what had happened to his companion. Had the man fallen to his death?

Faintly, from far below, he heard the Ta'amireh's voice. He had managed to get the flare lit, and Harding could see that his companion had fallen into a deep hole. It took time to help him out, and both men were thankful to wriggle back to fresh air, light and safety.

Cave Three also had a slanting cleft into its depths. Courageous Hasan Awad, the foreman of the workers from Qumran, had to be lowered down into it by ropes.

Hauling him back was a nightmare, since the sharp rocks threatened to cut the ropes in two.

Much was found in the four Wady Murabba'at caves, but nothing that linked them with Qumran. The Biblical fragments of Old Testament scrolls were of much later date. Nevertheless, the discoveries were noteworthy. Had they not been overshadowed by the importance of Qumran they would have received much more attention from the archaeological world.

The most wonderful were pottery shards, a sickle and blades, spearheads, buttons and a ring from the Chalcolithic Age, the period of about 4000 B.C., between the Stone and Copper ages. Amazingly, wood from that period had also survived in these dry caves. The shaft of an adze and a donkey goad were also found.

In addition Cave Two yielded bronze needles and an alabaster vase, dating from the seventeenth or eighteenth century B.C., and three of the caves contained objects from the eighth century B.C. The majority of the finds, however, were from the time of the Roman occupation, first and second centuries A.D., when the caves had been used by rebels and, later, perhaps by persecuted individuals or brigands.

The expedition lasted weeks, and although some of the Bedouins were helping at Wady Murabba'at, others of the tribe were taking advantage of Harding's and de Vaux's absence from Qumran. One of his workmen brought Harding the news.

Another scroll cave had been found by the Bedouins near the plateau.

The Director of Antiquities immediately left for Qumran. From the valley floor he could spot the dust clouds made by the hurried, illicit diggers. They were working in a spot quite close to the first cave discovery. Harding knew he had to move quickly if he was to prevent them from taking their finds away. He drove on as fast as he could to Jericho.

Here he found two men of the Arab Legion and returned with them to Qumran. The decision to bring soldiers with him was distasteful to Harding, but necessary. He was racing against time. He had to stop the Bedouins before they despoiled the cave.

These shy, secretive desert men trusted him enough to approach him, talk to him, and sell him what they found, but they still could not believe they would be paid unless scrolls and fragments were actually in their hands. Harding had explained to them that the fragile pieces must be handled expertly, kept between slides so their edges would not break. He had told them their sandals crushed valuable pieces into the cave floor.

His arguments were of no avail. The Bedouins obviously felt it better to risk destroying some pieces than not have any in their possession. It would have been futile for Harding to meet them at the cave, alone. In the delicate balance of friendship and authority he had to maintain, forcing the Bedouins into defying him openly would have been disastrous.

Despite his speed, he was too late. The Arab Legion soldiers caught four of the diggers, but the rest had vanished with the booty. The cave was stripped. From

141

the prisoners Harding learned there had been no complete scrolls or jars, but they remained obstinately silent on what had been taken away. He could only surmise there had been scroll fragments.

After questioning, the Bedouins were released with a stern warning that the tribe must bring everything to him or Saad. The price the government offered was more than fair, but Harding feared the Bethlehem dealers might promise more.

Since word had spread that the Metropolitan was asking a million dollars for the scrolls he had bought for two hundred and fifty, the dealers—including Kando—had hopes of richly profitable sales to wealthy, foreign, individual collectors, if more scrolls should be found.

Harding knew it was useless to pursue the Bedouins and dangerous to punish them. He would only drive them to hide their activities and their discoveries from him. He must wait and hope. He was grateful to them for their discoveries, but dismayed at the damage they did to the caves' precious contents.

The matter was discussed among the other archaeologists resident in the Jordan part of Jerusalem, and it was agreed they should organize a cave hunt of their own. It was a joint expedition, planned and financed by the American School of Oriental Research, the French Dominican Bible School, and the Palestine Museum as represented by Harding. The Jordan government was not a partner in this venture.

The explorations at Wady Murabba'at were finished, the excavations on the plateau were again postponed, and in the beginning of March, 1952, a full-scale search was launched in the mountains in the vicinity of Qumran.

For days they climbed, searching every likely hole, investigating an area of about ten miles north and south behind Qumran. They found thirty-seven caves, twenty-five of which contained broken shards of pottery, but no scrolls or fragments of scrolls. The expedition seemed a waste of time. They had found small scroll fragments in the cave the Bedouins had looted, but that was all.

Then, on March 14, they made a fantastic discovery. They found a cave with some scraps of scrolls and broken jars. They were about to conclude this was all when an assistant of Father de Vaux's, from the French Dominican School, spotted two large rolls far back against the cave wall. They turned out to be not leather but *copper* scrolls!

That they were scroll books was clear. The indentation of the writing on the inside was strong enough to show through. They were, however, impossible to unwind. Oxidation had made them so hard and brittle, they would have broken if forced. The scrolls were carefully coated with a celluloid solution and sent to the Palestine Museum until a decision could be made on the best method of opening them.

In handling the scrolls, though, it was discovered that the two were actually one scroll, which had broken apart at a riveted edge. It was estimated that the complete scroll would be about eight feet in length and twelve inches in width.

Four other caves were found, each containing a small amount of scroll fragments.

That was all. The expedition was over, but the finding

The two sections of the copper scroll found in Cave Three

of the strange copper scroll made the archaeologists feel well repaid for their time and money. It tantalized their curiosity, but they could not work with such fragile metal until engineering experts could show them the way.

Work was resumed at the Qumran excavations. And, to the archaeologists' relief, a steady trickle of scroll fragments, from the cave the Bedouins had discovered, made their way through dealers to Harding. Perhaps a few of those fragments went into the collections of wealthy foreigners, but both de Vaux and Harding were gaining confidence that the dealers were either not getting the huge prices they hoped for or the difficulties of evading the law were too great and the safest purchaser was the Department of Antiquities.

Their theory was borne out by what happened next.

On September 18, 1952, Father de Vaux was attending to some duties at the Dominican School, when two Bedouins were shown into the small room where he was working.

After the formal salutations the tribesmen said they had scroll pieces to sell. Did he want to buy them? Father de Vaux knew they meant the Department of Antiquities, and were using him as intermediary. Evidently they wanted a direct sale. They hoped both to eliminate a dealer's profit and to avoid a confrontation with Harding for despoiling the cave.

De Vaux hastily thought of what little money of his own he could advance. Sufficient or not, he must not hesitate. Yes, he told them, he'd buy what they had.

They went out and returned with a dozen more Bedouins, who had waited in the monastery garden. They were all carrying parcels, the contents of which they dumped on the table top in front of de Vaux.

For once the voluble Frenchman was speechless. He had expected a small number of fragments. Instead, the pile grew and grew as each Bedouin stepped up to add his share. Finally, rising a foot high, it covered the entire top of the table.

Harding was in Amman, and de Vaux had to act

quickly. He was able to raise thirteen hundred pounds, close to three thousand seven hundred dollars, for which he knew he would be repaid. He questioned the Bedouins and found that these fragments had come from still another new cave.

As soon as the Bedouins left he telephoned to Amman, and once again Harding raced to Qumran. There was the telltale cloud of dust around another cave, and another flight of Bedouins from the scene as his car was spotted. He did intercept a fresh relay of the tribe as they came to take their turn, and found out from them that they had been scooping fragments from the cave for three days, working in shifts.

The new cave was close to the excavations, but the entrance to it had been so small neither of the archaeologists had seen it.

Harding drove on to Jerusalem in a conflict of emotions—gratitude for the incredibly sharp eyes of the Bedouins and impotent despair at the disappearance of the fragments and the trampling of another cave.

He knew from de Vaux's telephone call that the latter had bought fragments, but he had no idea of how many. His friend met him at the Dominican School door and reassured him that, yes, he had purchased a few.

Joseph Saad was already there. With a fine sense of drama de Vaux led them both into the study and pointed to the table, enjoying their stupefaction at the tremendous pile.

Harding was, of course, delighted at the evidence that all the fragments were coming into the ownership of the

Department of Antiquities, but they presented a problem. Money would have to be found to repay de Vaux and to buy whatever else the Bedouins might have.

The Jordanian government was doing all it could to finance the treasure-trove, but its resources were limited and reaching an end. Harding raised a couple of thousand dollars by pledging Palestine Museum funds. For a little while he could satisfy the Bedouins but the Museum advance would have to be paid back. And if more caves were discovered—?

Too, there were now vast quantities of fragments to be assembled and translated. More scholars were needed, to work with Fathers Milik and Barthélemy and their services would have to be paid for.

CHAPTER VIII

WHILE HARDING SEARCHED for the best way of raising funds, he and de Vaux continued the excavation of the dwelling on the plateau. During their work an ancient oil lamp they found led them to the discovery of still another cave.

On September 22 a lamp was found in the diggings. It was old and corroded, but was still recognizable as a type of primitive oil lamp used two thousand years ago. As they were examining the lamp an elderly Arab workman drew near and inspected it carefully.

Finally he asked if they were interested in such objects. If so, he knew where there was one just like it, close by.

Father de Vaux grabbed his arm. "Uncle! If you know of one—where is it?" ("Uncle" was his term of affectionate respect for the elderly Arab.)

The old man would not be hurried. He had a story to tell. Squatting down on his heels, he began his rambling account. When he was a young man he'd been hunting partridges one day on this plateau. He had shot one and winged it, but it was still able to fly off and into a hole. Determined not to lose his dinner, he had followed it and crawled into the hole. There he had seen a lamp just like the one de Vaux was holding.

"But where is it?" he was asked.

He stood up and pointed to the left edge of the plateau. There was a small hole plainly visible from the site of the excavation.

The two archaeologists looked at each other. Day after day they had seen this hole. They had even joked about it, saying how convenient a storage place it would have been for the Essenes, if only that hole had led to a cave. But that was impossible. Caves were found in rock, not in marl and sand.

If the old man's memory was reliable, then there *was* a cavity behind that hole. If there was a lamp inside, then men had put it there.

Father de Vaux and a workman hung onto Harding's legs and lowered him, head-first, into the hole. They heard him shout, and when he re-emerged he was exultant. It was a cave, but he and de Vaux had been right. It was not a natural cavity but a man-made one. In it he had seen not only "Uncle's" lamp but a quantity of scroll fragments.

It became essential, now, that all the caves be numbered so that the fragments could be tagged according to the cave in which they were found, before they were sent to the Palestine Museum.

The Wady Murabba'at caves, One to Four, were kept in a separate category, as were the objects found in them.

Cave One of Qumran was, of course, the first discovery by the Bedouin boy. Cave Two was the one Harding had tried to save with the help of the Arab Legion soldiers; Cave Three was the one containing the copper scroll; from Cave Four had come the pile of fragments in de Vaux's study; Cave Five was the old Arab "uncle's" find.

Shortly after the discovery of Cave Five, the Bedouins located another containing a few fragments, and this was labeled Six. Caves Seven, Eight, Nine and Ten were the ones discovered during the archaeologists' own earlier cave hunt, though no great quantities of manuscript fragments had been found in them.

Even though Cave Six had not yielded much, the problem of money had grown acute. Fragments were still being offered for sale by Kando and other dealers, and by the Bedouins. All the resources Harding had at his disposal were overstrained.

Harding had personal authority for disbursements of the trust fund for the Palestine Museum. He spent nearly $183,000 of Museum funds to buy scroll fragments, to pay the transcribers at the Museum, and to help pay for the excavations at Qumran. The government allotment for the Department of Antiquities had long been spent, and the endowment funds could not be drained further without making the operation of the Museum suffer. Yet a lot more money was needed.

The archaeologists wanted to recruit men—Bible scholars, paleographers, historians and language experts

*View showing entrance to Cave Four (upper right), which
contained one of the richest finds of scroll fragments*

—from all over the world, and bring them to Jerusalem as a team to sort and transcribe the many thousands of fragments. They hoped for young men, to encourage them in their professions.

It was already being said that the Dead Sea Scrolls were stirring the imagination of young people. Universities were reporting an increased interest in archaeology, a realization that the science was not only concerned with fossils and bones but also involved romance and mystery.

Such a team of scholars would be expensive. The participants would have to be paid and housed, and would need the best equipment.

Harding's final decision was not an easy one. Sentiment urged that all the work be done in Jerusalem, but he could not ask money from foreign institutions and give nothing in return. The situation forced him to be practical. He offered the museums and universities of other nations sections of pieced-together scrolls for cash. They were requested to pay first and then wait until the transcriptions were completed, photographed, and published before they could take actual possession of the scrolls, or scroll fragments.

He was criticized for this action by those who felt that such a great historical treasure should not be disposed of in bits and pieces. There was another consideration in favor of Harding's plan. Should another war or an earthquake strike Jerusalem, the entire collection might be destroyed in one day.

McGill University, in Canada, offered fifteen thousand

dollars, the gift of a woman donor, for scroll fragments; Manchester University, three thousand dollars; the Vatican Library contributed more than twenty thousand. McCormick Theological Seminary in Chicago bought some fragments from Cave Four, and almost fifteen thousand dollars came from the University of Heidelberg in Germany. Other national institutions and universities bought what they could.

The total sum was enough to insure the continuation of plans and purchases. No special scrolls could be earmarked for any one donor, but each would be given sections commensurate with their purchase money.

In January of 1953 a call went out to many national scientific institutions and universities for names of qualified men. Each expert chosen must be willing to continue as a member of the team for a period of years and to sustain his particular project until it was completed. The work was too intricate for frequent changes in personnel.

Insofar as it was possible, since the work demanded a high degree of expert knowledge, the final choices were made from a wide selection of nationalities and from among younger men.

In May the team assembled in Jerusalem. Lodgings were found for them either in the American School of Oriental Research building, the Dominican School, or in private quarters.

They gathered in the Palestine Museum and introduced themselves. They were Dr. Frank Cross and Father Patrick Skehan, from America; Father Jean Starcky of Poland; Dr. Claus Hunzinger, Germany; John Strugnell and John M. Allegro, England. Father Milik, born in Poland, but now of French nationality, would be part of the team, but Father Barthélemy had been flown out for medical treatment. The eyestrain had been too much for him.

Father de Vaux would supervise when he was not at Qumran, and Joseph Saad was to be responsible for the physical set-up of the rooms where the team would work. These rooms were dubbed the "Scrollery."

The new men gathered behind Milik's chair at the long table in the largest room. He showed them the pieces he was working on, a jigsaw-puzzle arrangement of tiny fragments which, unfortunately, did not fit together as neatly as a jigsaw. Two fragments might fit at the top but not at the bottom, leaving a gap of a letter or a word.

Milik explained that these fragments were part of a Formulary of Blessings. It gave instructions on the manner in which the Essenes were to bless, or greet, different groups among them. There were blessings for the High Priest, for other priests, for laymen, even for the king, since the sect believed that a king-Messiah as well as a priestly one was to come.

The work was not complete. Father Milik was still searching for fragments belonging to it. It might turn out to be a complete scroll or only a portion of one. Even in what he had already gathered together, words and whole lines were missing.

The team was shown the photography laboratory, the small library with its stacks of reference books for their use, the typewriters and other equipment, even the smocks supplied for them to wear when they handled dusty leather fragments.

They examined the cabinets whose shallow drawers held hundreds of scroll pieces, and the flat boxes of hundreds more, still uncleaned, the recent purchases from the Bedouins, labeled only by the caves from which they had come.

And, last, they stood in wonder before the copper scroll, its mystery still retained within its unopened metal rolls.

Although most of the leather pieces were unclassified, a sample categorizing had been done so the team knew, in a general way, what they could expect to find. They agreed to divide up the work.

Dr. Frank Cross and Father Patrick Skehan were to concentrate on the Old Testament books. John Allegro

John Allegro piecing together a first-century commentary on the Book of Nahum

was given the Biblical commentaries; John Strugnell, the hymn scrolls; while Dr. Claus Hunziger was to begin work on the War Scrolls, copies of which were turning up. Father Milik was to finish the Formulary of Blessings, and then search for scrolls on astronomy, in which the sect seemed to have taken a keen interest. Father Jean Starcky would work only on those scrolls written in Aramaic. This was the language of the common people at the time of Christ, and was the language of some of the scrolls.

The Museum sheltered another scholar, Father Maurice Baillet, who was to work separately on cataloguing the material taken from the Wady Murabba'at caves, and on transcribing the writings found there.

Eager as they were to begin, the Scrollery team was appalled at the difficulties facing them.

The Bedouins had cleaned out each cave by gathering all the fragments together, collecting them in sacks, cigarette cartons or cigar boxes. If the archaeologists could have entered an untouched cave, they would have made some selection on the spot. It would have been reasonable to assume that fragments in one square foot might be parts of the same scroll that had disintegrated. Not only would these fragments have been put in one box and labeled, but the squares adjoining them would also have been marked, in case they should overlap.

But now, in front of each team worker were unsorted pieces under glass, or simply a pile of tiny fragments if they had just come from the Bedouins. Each single scrap had to be identified, classified, sorted; some had to be cleaned and prepared first. The task was staggering. As

Reverend Joseph Fitzmyer, one of the indexers, making a first examination of scroll fragments

the weeks went by they looked with something akin to dread upon Joseph Saad whenever he entered the Scrollery with newly purchased boxes of scroll material.

Kando and the Bedouins seemed to follow no orderly method in their selling, because the fragments might be from Cave Two or Cave Six or any of the others, except for the very first.

Each small leather piece had to be dusted first with a

The Scrollery tables on which the tens of thousands of frag-ments were laid out so that the scrolls could be pieced together

fine camel's-hair brush; if the dust still clung, the brush would be dipped in castor oil. This was also done when the writing was illegible; the oil made the leather trans-lucent and brought out the letters and words.

Many of the tiny fragments could not go immediately under glass. The leather had curled, become dry and brittle, or the edges were rolled over. To try to flatten them would only break them. These were put into a large glass jar. At the bottom was a space for water, covered by a perforated zinc plate. The fragments rested on the zinc, the lid was sealed, and the jar put in a warm place. The jar had to be watched carefully, or the humidity would soften the fragments into a glue-like substance or even liquefy them into a glob of brown jelly.

Carefully supervised, the hard, brittle leather would soften just enough to uncurl and straighten, and could be easily handled. Stubbornly rigid fragments might need a second treatment, but ten or fifteen minutes of one humidity bath was usually enough.

As the work progressed and more glass slides were filled, more table space was needed. Eventually two long parallel tables, on trestles, went the full length of the big room. Additional smaller tables were set up when necessary.

It was a quiet place. The work demanded intense concentration. Even the frequent movements of one or another of the workers, walking down the length of the tables, peering at slide after slide as he tried to find a matching piece, was done as noiselessly as possible so as not to distract the others.

The easiest pieces to find were those written in Aramaic. All of these went to Father Jean Starcky. Gradually the other team members found small clues which would help them, too. Scrolls differed in color, because of the various shades of goat and sheepskin. Some scribes had very distinctive handwritings. One might have used a thick pen; another a very dark ink. Most of the scribes had individual peculiarities: a fast, sprawling hand, or tight, neat lettering.

What was maddening was that, just as a Scrollery worker became familiar with the idiosyncrasies of a scroll, it might change. The scribe might start using a different

An ordinary photograph of a scroll fragment

An infrared photograph of the same fragment

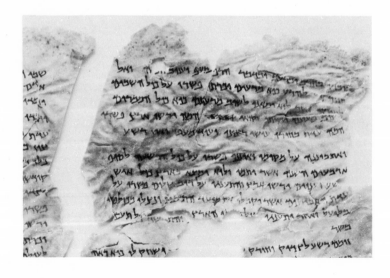

pen or ink, or a new section meant to be sewn to the last might be of a yellowish leather instead of brown.

Equal to the physical demands upon eyes and backs and shoulders was the trial of scholarship. It was not enough to know ancient Hebrew. When a scholar must supply a word or phrase he must be fully aware of what the scribe was trying to copy. This meant constant recourse to the historical and religious treatises dealing with the centuries of the Essenes.

The most difficult fragments were those written in code. The Essenes considered some of their writings as too private to put into "clear" Hebrew. The team members had to break the codes, which were chiefly alphabetical ciphers, before they could get on with transcribing. Letters written backward were another code. Some scrolls, though mainly written in Hebrew, would have code words inserted.

Fragments that were too black from age and humidity were taken to the photographic laboratory. Here Mr. Mejid Anton Albina presided. After much experimentation he had found that he could get the best results with his infrared films and plates by setting the camera about thirty-two inches from the glass slides of scroll pieces.

For the extremely darkened leather he used an exposure of eight minutes; for the less discolored pieces only four to six minutes.

The results seemed magical. The infrared film plainly showed the words or letters on leather where no writing could be seen before.

The Scrollery workers found that the majority of the

fragments were copies of Old Testament books, although there were some original writings of the sect. Cave Two yielded portions of the books of Jeremiah, Exodus, Leviticus, Numbers, Deuteronomy, Ruth and Psalms. A fragment of the book of Jubilees, a religious work long known, though not from the Bible, was also found there.

From Cave Four came the largest mass of scroll pieces, sixty copies of Bible books, and a Commentary on the Psalms written by an Essene author in the manner of the Habakkuk Commentary. The Psalm Commentary repeated the Essenic philosophy of the victory of the good over the wicked and the meek over their enemies.

Part of the Book of Tobit (better known as the Book of Tobias), one of the Apocrypha, which is still included in the Roman Catholic Bible as "deuterocanonical," was found in Cave Five.

Eventually the work of the Scrollery would present for publication every book of the Old Testament, and many copies of some, but with one notable exception. That was the Book of Esther. Its exclusion raised many questions to which no answer has yet been found.

In the first year of their labor the Scrollery team were glad of an occasional chance to get away from the tables and from staring at leather scraps which might be less than an inch long. As often as possible they borrowed a car and drove out along the eastward pass from Jerusalem to Qumran.

All through the spring, summer and autumn of 1953 work had progressed on the settlement building. They had excavated beyond the big central courtyard, which separated the main council hall, dining room, scriptorium, kitchen and watchtower from another complex of smaller rooms and cisterns.

A pottery kiln had been found. The men of Qumran, Harding explained, had evidently made their own pottery dishes and jars. This partly explained why the jars were of a different shape from the usual ones of Palestine, though it did not explain why they happened to resemble jars from Egypt of that time.

The Scrollery scholars had many questions to ask. What had the settlement lived on? Where did they get water? Approximately how many people had lived on the plateau at one time?

Although their number might have fluctuated over the long period of exile, the archaeologists estimated from the size of the building and the quantity of dishes that about two hundred men usually lived there. There were no sleeping quarters inside the building. It would be normal then, as it still is in that climate, for the men to sleep out of doors, in tents or, during winter storms, in caves or any rock shelter. All they needed for beds would be reed mats that could be rolled up in the daytime.

Here and there on the plateau were the black tents of the Arab workmen, and the visitors could picture from them what Qumran had once looked like with tents for two hundred men dotting the plateau outside the walls.

How had the community lived? Possibly, de Vaux said, they had sold pottery in Jericho, about seven miles north. But they would have had little use for money. They could get salt from the Dead Sea, meat, milk and cheese from

|163

their goats. At the pool of Ain Feshka they probably grew grain for bread and flax for cloth. The flax was made into clothing, the "spotless white robes" they put on for communal meals, as well as their ordinary work clothes. It also made the napkins with which they dried themselves after purification, and the linen coverings for the scrolls.

There was some evidence that palm trees had once flourished around the Ain Feshka oasis; from those trees would have come dates for eating and the material for roofing the building and its annexes. A settled community would have planted fruit trees, and they might have kept bees for honey.

The same leather, of goat or sheep hide, which made the scrolls would also have been tanned for sandals, pouches, thongs and ropes, perhaps even shields for defense, and shirts to wear in cold weather.

Olive trees need little moisture. If the pool at Ain Feshka had been dammed, where now it trickled uselessly into the Dead Sea, it would have irrigated a fairly large cultivated area at the edge of which the sect could have planted olive trees to supply them with food, and oil for their lamps.

But, asked the Scrollery workers, looking about them at the arid plateau, how could two hundred men live in such a place without water? It could possibly have been carried up from Ain Feshka for drinking purposes but not in sufficient quantities, surely, for the emphasis on bathing?

The two archaeologists led the group around the en-

164|

tire excavation, pointing out a very large cistern, or reservoir, outside the walls, two others in the southeast corner of the building, a well-built septic tank, and the bathing pools. They admitted that they, too, had been puzzled by where the water had come from to fill them.

Harding pointed to a number of dry grooves cutting

A typical cistern. The plaster on many of them is still in good condition.

A water tunnel through a cliff, part of the elaborate conduit system that supplied the Qumran community

across the floor of the big courtyard, outlined by stones. "These channels baffled us at first," he said. "They meandered in every direction. Father de Vaux almost had apoplexy, trying to understand their purpose. Eventually we realized that they were part of an intricate conduit system that brought in water to the settlement from the mountain."

Guided by Harding, the visitors followed the maze of channels until they merged into one larger aqueduct outside the building. The aqueduct continued on to the head of Wady Qumran, a gorge in the mountain. Here the Essenes had tunneled through rock for several yards to tap a hidden spring.

The cisterns would also have captured and stored the winter rain water. The largest one had a settling basin into which the water ran and was cleared before it flowed under the walls. All had well-plastered steps leading down into them, so that the water was accessible no matter how low the level fell.

The visitors climbed to the top of the watchtower. From here the community had kept a lookout for enemies or conducted their astronomical observations. The Scrollery team looked downward onto the excavated rooms and courtyards and, in imagination, saw them peopled with the grave, bearded men of the sect.

More information had been added to that contained in the Manual of Discipline. This came from a document called the Damascus Covenant, discovered in a Cairo synagogue in 1896 by the Jewish scholar Solomon Schechter, a lecturer in England's University of Cambridge. Schechter's manuscript of the Damascus Covenant dated from the ninth century.

As far back as 1948 in Jerusalem, when Dr. Burrows examined the Manual of Discipline with Trever and Brownlee, he had noted a connection of this Qumran scroll with the Damascus Covenant. Before Dr. Sukenik died in 1952 he had suggested the Covenant was an

|167

Essenic book, copied and recopied for eight centuries. The Covenant had been a historical curiosity since its discovery in the nineteenth century, because it described some of the religious philosophy and ritual life of an unknown sect.

Now a careful comparison between the Damascus Covenant and the Manual of Discipline showed word-for-word agreement in several passages, as well as in the statement of religious principles. The relationship between the Damascus Covenant and the Qumran scrolls was confirmed by the finding, in Cave Six, of an older copy of the Covenant, proving Burrows' and Sukenik's theory correct.

It cannot yet be explained how or why this Covenant found its way to Egypt, and how or why a copy had been preserved until its discovery in 1896, but it does show that not all the exciting detective work was being done at the excavation site. Some of it was taking place in the quiet atmosphere of study rooms.

The Damascus Covenant claimed, as a reason for the exile, that only the members of the priestly order of the Sons of Zadok could qualify as High Priests in Jerusalem. Some scholars considered this as proof that persecution of the Teacher began when the Hasmonean king, Alexander Jannaeus, usurped the role of the rightful High Priests.

The Scrollery team debated this, as they did other theories, during rest periods, strolling through the Museum's handsome lecture theater, galleries, reading rooms and record rooms and down cool corridors where brown walnut doors made a striking contrast to the white limestone walls. Their favorite gathering place was the Museum cloister. Here a rectangular pool in the center was open to the sky, but the paved walks around it were sheltered from the sun by protective arcades.

Was Alexander Jannaeus the Wicked Priest? If so, it would be logical that an unknown Teacher of Righteousness would proclaim that the Temple was being defiled when Jannaeus' bloody hands were the ones to offer the priestly sacrifice. The teacher would surely be persecuted for taking such a stand.

Father de Vaux felt this was still an unproved theory. But on another subject—the identity of the Kittim—de Vaux and Yigael Yadin as well as many other scholars were by now convinced that Kittim referred to the Romans. A group of fragments from Cave Four had turned out to be a commentary on the prophet Nahum. One passage in it read, in part: "Kings of Greece from Antiochus until the appearance of the rulers of the Kittim." Scholars had wondered if the Kittim were the earlier Greek oppressors, or the later Roman ones. This particular passage bolstered the Roman-Kittim theory (and would date the scrolls to that later period) because it distinctly stated that Kittim came after the Greeks.

CHAPTER IX

On the other side of the armistice barrier that cut Jerusalem in two, Yigael Yadin carried on the work of his father, the late Dr. Sukenik. In 1950 Yadin had been able to put aside his military uniform and devote himself to his true vocation of archaeology.

He had sympathized deeply with his father's disappointment that the Metropolitan's four scrolls had slipped from his grasp. Dr. Sukenik had been so close to buying them, when Mar Athanasius had changed his mind and taken them to America. Just as, in Jordan, it was felt that all the scrolls should remain there because they were found there, so in Israel it was thought that they belonged in Israel, since they were part of Jewish history and heritage.

In January of 1954 Professor Yadin received an invitation to make an extended lecture tour of the United States. The invitation reminded him again of those four scrolls. They were in America—but what had happened to them? There had been no announcement made of their sale.

He arrived in New York, and for four months traveled about, lecturing at institutions and at private functions.

On May 27 he spoke at Johns Hopkins University, where he met Professor William F. Albright. They chatted awhile, and then Professor Yadin asked why the American Schools of Oriental Research had never published anything from the Metropolitan's fourth scroll, the small one that was gummed together.

Professor Albright replied that the Metropolitan had withdrawn permission from the A.S.O.R. and Harvard University to unroll it. He would neither allow it to be photographed nor agree to the publication of its text until all four scrolls had found a buyer.

"Why don't the Americans buy the scrolls?" asked Yadin. "Surely a few million dollars for such a purpose is not too difficult to raise."

The answer astounded him. The Metropolitan would probably, by now, be willing to sell them for half a million or less, but there were no buyers. The chief reason for this was the clouded title to the scrolls. Individuals like Anton Kiraz, even Kando, were claiming part ownership, and the government of Jordan had made it clear they considered the Metropolitan's possession of the scrolls illegal.

If this were so, Yadin asked, why shouldn't he try to buy them for Israel? He felt no one had a better right to ancient Jewish manuscripts than the new Jewish state.

But when Professor Albright said he would try to get the Metropolitan's address for him, Professor Yadin demurred.

A direct approach might be the wrong one. If he were too precipitous and it became known he was the buyer, Jordan might take legal action that would entangle the Metropolitan and might embarrass not only Israel but the United States.

Professor Yadin continued his lecture tour, but those four scrolls were constantly on his mind. It was irksome to feel he must be cautious, and no roundabout approach suggested itself to him.

At the same time, Mar Athanasius was coming to a decision of his own.

He had been bitterly disappointed by his failure to make a sale. He had been hurt by the imputations that he was not the legal owner of the scrolls. He had been subjected to notoriety in the newspapers. There were scholars who still doubted the age or authenticity of the scrolls and called them a hoax. An article written just the past year had referred to the scrolls as "St. Mark's garbage."

His work in helping the Syrian churches in the Western Hemisphere had been successful. A new cathedral had been consecrated in New Jersey, and named St. Mark's after the monastery in Jerusalem. If not for the problem of disposing of the scrolls, he would have been content. America was now his home.

And because he had refused to extend his agreement with the American Schools of Oriental Research for publication of the scrolls, they were costing money for insurance and storage. He had set up trustees and a trust fund, to allocate the proceeds from any sale of the scrolls for charitable purposes, yet he had not been able to sell them.

In May of 1954, while Professor Yadin was making his lecture tour, Mar Athanasius heard that McGill University had bought a number of fragments from Jordan and had paid fifteen thousand dollars for them. This was the sale Harding had arranged to help pay for the Scrollery work.

Fifteen thousand dollars for some fragments alone, and the Metropolitan had four entire scrolls! It was time, he felt, to take more positive action. He decided to advertise.

On the first of June Professor Yadin, in New York City, received a telephone call. It was from a newspaper friend, Mr. Monty Jacobs. Had Yadin seen the *Wall Street Journal* that day?

Yadin was amused. No, he hadn't seen it; he wasn't planning to buy any stocks and bonds.

Mr. Jacobs explained. There was an advertisement in the paper offering the Dead Sea Scrolls for sale. Mr. Jacobs, hoping for a journalistic scoop, thought that an archaeologist like Professor Yadin might be able to give him the reasons and the background for such a sale—

Yadin interrupted him, asking him to bring the *Wall Street Journal* to his hotel immediately. He waited impatiently until the newspaperman arrived. Then both pored over a small advertisement buried on a back page. It read:

Professor Yadin was scarcely able to believe his eyes. It
seemed a miracle that the advertisement should appear
just at this moment, and that his attention should be
called to it. What seemed disgraceful to him was that
the Dead Sea Scrolls should have to be hawked like
second-hand automobiles or furniture, in the columns of
a newspaper. Although the advertisement did not mention the Metropolitan, the scrolls must be his.

The archaeologist said nothing of his hopes to the
journalist, but promised to find out what he could. Monty
Jacobs would get his story, but at this point he must say
nothing to his own editors, and not call attention to the
ad in the *Wall Street Journal*.

In fact, the advertisement seemed to have gone almost
unnoticed. No other newspaper picked it up. It inspired
no new headline stories on the scrolls. This fact gave
Yadin time to think out a way to approach the Metropolitan. He hoped to find a proxy buyer, a businessman
he could trust, but who would not be associated with
the State of Israel. Yadin did not even get in touch with
the Hebrew University or officials in Israel. That could
wait.

He talked the problem over with Mr. T. Bennahum, a businessman, and a relative of Yadin's wife. How would he handle the matter? A banker friend of Mr. Bennahum's was taken into their confidence. The banker sent a letter to the *Wall Street Journal*, asking for more information about the advertised Dead Sea Scrolls, on behalf of one of the bank's customers. The letter stated that necessary arrangements would have to be made for an expert to examine the scrolls before the sale negotiations proceeded.

Days went by. There was no answer. Professor Yadin could hardly contain his impatience and worry. Perhaps the advertisement had caught other eyes? Supposing the Metropolitan was besieged by potential buyers? Was he going to lose out, as his father had in 1948?

Then the banker telephoned: a reply had come. It was a cordial letter, which included a description and history of the scrolls, and suggested a meeting date. The letter was signed by Charles Manoog, and it ended with an unintentional bit of irony: "Will you please inform me if your client has some realization of their historical value and worth or shall it be advisable for me to send you more references regarding these documents?"

There was no question of this prospective buyer not knowing their worth. Professor Yadin was completely satisfied, after reading the description, that the scrolls were indeed the Metropolitan's, and he was determined to have them for Israel.

The Metropolitan was in Florida, so the viewing of the scrolls would have to wait for his return, but the negotiations continued. Mr. Manoog and Mr. Bennahum met. The latter reported to Professor Yadin that the price was very high. A four-hundred-thousand-dollar figure had been mentioned for only one scroll. However, the two men conferred again and again, and finally Mr. Manoog said he was authorized, on behalf of the Metropolitan, to accept two hundred and fifty thousand dollars for all four scrolls.

It was a very reasonable price, but now Professor Yadin had to think of how to raise the money. Eventually Israel would be the owner, but he must move quickly to be able to pay for the scrolls.

He spoke to several people whose discretion he could trust. They were amazed at such a stroke of good fortune, and were certain a loan could be arranged. But it would take time, and Professor Yadin did not have much time.

The Metropolitan would be returning soon. If Yadin's emissary could not produce the two hundred and fifty thousand dollars, the deal would fall through.

Mr. Izhak Norman, director of the American Fund for Israel Institutions, came to the rescue. He would lend money out of the Fund's Treasury if Professor Yadin could get the Israeli government to guarantee it. Thus far Yadin had not mentioned the scrolls to officials in Israel. He now cabled the Director-General of the Prime Minister's office, Mr. Teddy Kolleck:

"An unexpected miracle has happened. The Four Dead Sea Scrolls, including Isaiah, brought to U.S. by the Syrian Metropolitan, are offered for sale. They can be bought at once for $250,000. No need to stress the importance of the scrolls and the unrepeatable opportunity. And delay may ruin our chance. Have already probed several important donors, and consider it certain that the sum may be collected within a year. A guarantee from the Treasury for the whole sum is imperative. Request your immediate action with the PM [Prime Minister] and Minister of Finance. Secrecy imperative. Yigael."

For two days Professor Yadin's spirits veered between hope and moments of despair. He knew the government would want the scrolls, but Israel was a new country and financial problems pressed in upon it.

Toward the close of the second day the answer came:

"The Prime Minister and Minister of Finance are delighted with the wonderful opportunity. Orders for suitable guarantees have been dispatched. Mazel-tov!—Teddy."

Mazel-tov!—the word for congratulations. A great burden lifted off Professor Yadin's shoulders. For the first time he allowed himself to believe that the sale would go through.

There were still anxious moments. The sale deed had been drawn up, waiting for signatures, by June 18, but the Metropolitan was still in Florida. He would not fly, so his trip back to New York would be further delayed.

Then Mr. Bennahum left for Europe and another proxy for Yadin had to be found. The business associate of Mr. Bennahum, Mr. Sydney Estridge, took over.

Word came from Mr. Manoog that the Metropolitan would not arrive until June 30. In the tension of waiting, Professor Yadin was almost grateful for a lecture date which took him out of New York on June 28. He spoke before the America-Israel Society at the Library of Congress in Washington. His subject was "New Light on the Dead Sea Scrolls."

The plane took Yadin back to New York and into turmoil. A cablegram was waiting. It contained one word—"Well?"—from Teddy Kolleck, but it was enough to tell him that the tension was as great in Israel as in New York.

Mr. Estridge telephoned. The meeting was postponed until July 1, to enable the Metropolitan to get the scrolls out of the vault. But had Professor Yadin forgotten about getting an expert to look at them? Since this had been the buyer's request, it would look strange if Mr. Estridge suddenly seemed to care nothing about making sure of the scrolls' authenticity.

The Metropolitan arrived in New York while Professor Yadin was frantically trying to find a Hebrew language expert, whom he could pledge to secrecy. On July 1 Mar Athanasius, Mr. Manoog, and their lawyer met at the Waldorf-Astoria with Mr. Estridge and his lawyer. At one o'clock Mr. Estridge called to say that sale agreements were almost complete and that he and the lawyers were waiting for the expert to check the scrolls. Where was he?

At that frantic moment Yadin remembered a friend of his, Professor Harry Orlinsky, who was familiar with the texts of the scrolls. He phoned, and reached Orlinsky just as he was about to leave on a Canadian holiday with his family. All Yadin could say was that this was a desperate emergency. He asked his friend to come immediately to the hotel.

Professor Orlinsky rushed over, thinking some tragedy had occurred. But when he learned the Dead Sea Scrolls were for sale to Israel, and he was being asked to identify them, he was overjoyed, and gladly postponed his vacation. He took with him to the meeting at the Waldorf-Astoria facsimiles of the Metropolitan's scrolls.

All this had taken time. At the Waldorf-Astoria the lawyers discussed the last fine point of the legal wording of the contract as they waited. The Metropolitan sat in dignified silence, taking no part in the legal arrangements. He seemed to be remote and unemotional in his long black robes and bishop's miter.

He was later to write a book, in which he made it clear that inwardly he had been profoundly moved that day. On the table beside him lay the three transparent perspex boxes, through which he could see the scrolls of Isaiah, the Habakkuk Commentary and the Manual of Discipline. The still rolled up and untranscribed scroll lay in a separate wooden box. So much worry and triumph, hope and disappointment, had come to him since he had first laid eyes on the scrolls in the monastery in Jerusalem; now, in a matter of hours, they would pass from his possession to a stranger's.

The Metropolitan's thoughts were abruptly interrupted by the arrival of the expert. Professor Orlinsky introduced himself as "Mr. Green." This was a precaution, since it might possibly be known that Orlinsky was a friend of Yigael Yadin's. "Mr. Green" gently lifted each of the three scrolls from its plastic box, in turn, spread it out on the table and compared it with its facsimile in Dr. Burrows' book. At last he looked up and nodded.

These were the authentic Dead Sea Scrolls.

The Metropolitan had walked to the window and stood looking out upon the city streets. He wrote later that he felt certain the purchaser was an American who would make a gift of the scrolls to an American institution, and he was consoled; he had come to love his adopted country.

He was called for his signature. In a matter of minutes the transaction was finished. He saw the check for two hundred and fifty thousand dollars change hands. The Metropolitan had already decided that the money was to go into the "Archbishop Samuel Trust," a Syrian charitable fund.

The next morning Professor Yadin and his wife, with Mr. Estridge, drove to the Waldorf-Astoria, took the scrolls from the hotel safe and brought them back to Yadin's hotel. They were sealed in a small trunk. It was decided that the trunk should be officially opened at the Israeli Consulate, and the patient newspaperman, Monty Jacobs, was invited to be present.

While they waited for him Yadin sent the following wire to Israel: "To Teddy Kolleck, for the Prime Minister, Minister of Finances and President of the Hebrew University. For the difficulties that are now facing you, find consolation! The treasures of the past are in our hands as from [sic] this morning at 10:30. Will send them to Jerusalem next week. . . ."

At the Consulate that afternoon the trunk was opened in Monty Jacobs' presence and he was told the full story. It was not to be published, however, until the Israeli government made its official announcement of the purchase of the Dead Sea Scrolls.

Each scroll was sent to Israel separately. Professor Yadin had to go to England but he arranged to be notified in code of their arrival. The cables came while he was still on board ship. By the time he reached London all four scrolls were safe in the Hebrew University in Jerusalem.

The small brown scroll was unrolled at last. Years before, when it had first been brought to America, a small fragment had come loose and John C. Trever had glimpsed the writing on it. Because he made out the name "Lamech" it had acquired the name of the Lamech scroll, but now it was found to be a document in Aramaic based on the book of Genesis.

It was not a copy of Genesis, as the Isaiah scroll was a copy of the book of Isaiah. It contained many of the well-known stories from Genesis, but written in a different style, and interspersed with unknown details and new names. One of its odd features appeared toward the end of the scroll, where the account of Abraham's journey in Egypt is not told in the usual third person, but in the first person: "And I, Abram, went forth, exceedingly rich in cattle and also in silver and in gold, and I went up out of Egypt. . . ."

It would seem, in this scroll, that some ancient scribe had taken the literary liberty of imagining what Abraham's own thoughts and words had been.

The Israeli government formed a Shrine of the Book Trust. Its purpose was to build a special room at the Hebrew University to house these scrolls, and the three scrolls and jars Dr. Sukenik had purchased. All the major treasures gathered from the first cave found by the Bedouins were now together in one place. The special room

The Shrine of the Book in Jerusalem

even had an electronic device which would automatically lower the scrolls into a vault below ground, in case of fire or other danger to the building.

In February of 1955 the Israeli government formally announced to the world the acquisition of the Metropolitan's scrolls, and Monty Jacobs' patience was rewarded. He could at last publish the full, inside story.

The Metropolitan read about it with amazement. So the purchaser was really the state of Israel! Nevertheless, in the Metropolitan's book, *Treasure of Qumran*, he expressed his pleasure that the scrolls were now housed in the beautiful Shrine of the Book room, and said, "The scrolls are beacons in the night of vanished centuries. May they burn brightly forever along the road to Truth!"

CHAPTER X

De VAUX AND HARDING, in the fall of 1954, uncovered three small pottery jars near the southern walls of the excavation. The jars were filled with silver coins. The simplest explanation was that these constituted the treasury of the sect, since members had to surrender their money on joining.

But this was only a guess. And excited as they were by this new find, the archaeologists were even more intrigued by the still unsolved mystery of another metal treasure in their possession.

The copper scroll had remained at the Museum for all of 1953 and 1954, the object of much discussion. It had been coated with paraffin for preservation, but the edges were so brittle they broke at touch. It could not be unrolled. Another method would have to be found.

Any plan must be agreed upon by the three organizations who had financed the cave hunt that had yielded the scroll; that is, by the American School of Oriental Research, the Dominican Bible and Archaeological School, and the Palestine Museum. Representing the Museum, Harding had the task of finding the best method and the money needed to carry it out.

Various proposals had been made. Some seemed sensible; others were wildly impractical. One idea was to slip sensitized film inside the roll in the hope of recording the writing. Another was to plunge both parts of the scroll into a bath of liquid gold. The theory behind this was that gold, as a soft metal, would form a pliable sheet that would cling to the copper and allow it to be unrolled.

Such ideas were dismissed as impractical. For a while it seemed the Johns Hopkins University in Baltimore might have the solution, since they were working on ways of reconstituting corroded metal, but the copper scroll was so completely oxidized their method would not work.

It was finally agreed that the scroll would have to be cut into strips, not unrolled, so the problem became one of finding metal engineering experts to do the job.

During the three years the scroll had rested in the Museum, the imprints of words which showed through to the outside had lured and tantalized scholars. They were extremely difficult to read, since the words were, of course, in reverse. Nor did it help matters that the scrolls were kept under glass. One German professor, K. G. Kuhn, studied the indentations for a long time, under a powerful magnifying glass, and claimed he could read them.

Some of the words he deciphered were: "four . . . cubits . . . dig six cubits until the . . . eight cubits . . . the opening . . . gold." His report stirred some wild conjectures. Did the scroll contain the instructions for digging under some building? And what of that word: *gold*? But not much credence was given to Professor Kuhn's reading; jokes were made about what the fierce Jerusalem heat could do, even to responsible scholars.

In the spring of 1955 Harding was corresponding with several laboratories, when John Allegro suggested that the University of Manchester in England, where he had earned his own Honors degree in Oriental History, be entrusted with the cutting. He knew their laboratory equipment and technical skills. In May Harding wrote Allegro, who was visiting England, to make the necessary inquiries.

Dr. B. V. Bowden, principal of the Manchester College of Technology, was enthusiastic. He offered every laboratory facility, and persuaded Professor H. Wright Baker, of the Department of Mechanical Engineering, to take charge. Professor Baker immediately began the planning and construction of a special machine for the one purpose of cutting the copper scroll.

Allegro reported this to Harding when he returned to Jerusalem. It was felt the scroll could not be in better hands, and on July 13, 1955, Harding took the smaller of the two halves of the scroll to Manchester, after getting government permission to remove it from Jordan.

In September John Allegro was sent to England to work with Professor Baker. His first look at Baker's machine did not impress him favorably. It was a weird contraption. The scholars in Jerusalem had speculated on the modern electronic wonders Allegro would find for the cutting in the Manchester laboratory, but this was a homemade machine constructed out of bits of old metal and wood and string. There was even a knot in the string that ran from motor to saw, through a pulley wheel, and every time the knot passed through the pulley the whole machine bounced.

On close observation, however, it could be seen that Dr. Baker had wrought a sensible, clever device. The machine was made to fit the problems of the scroll.

The entire cutting apparatus was attached to a short track, similar to a train track, which was bolted to a table. It could thus easily be slid back and forth when required. From the base of the apparatus rose two upright metal arms, placed a little farther apart than the length of the scroll. At the top of each upright was a U-shaped "cradle" to hold a horizontal spindle. The spindle would, hopefully, fit inside the scroll. The U-shaped cradles would hold the spindle firmly, without slipping, but allow it to revolve. Suspended above, by string and pulley, was a tiny, circular saw, like a dental instrument, two inches in diameter, but only .006 inches thick. It could be lowered or raised at the slightest touch and because it hung on string instead of rigid metal, it could be moved and turned in the most delicate of manipulations, to cut around a letter instead of straight through it.

Also from the string and pulley there hung a magnifying glass, through which Dr. Baker could examine the scroll and be better able to guide the saw.

*Dr. H. Wright Baker and the ingenious machine he devised
for cutting the copper scroll*

When John Allegro first saw the apparatus, only the
thin metal spindle rested in the cradle of the uprights.
Before doing anything else, Dr. Baker coated the outside
of the copper scroll with Araldite plastic, an aircraft ad-
hesive, and then baked it for several hours. This
coating gave the corroded metal a pliable "skin." It was
hoped thus to prevent the scroll from crumbling or
splitting.

Then, with infinite care, the spindle was inserted down

the center of the scroll. It went in easily, relieving the worries of both Dr. Baker and Allegro, who had feared some corrosion of the copper might obstruct it.

The ends of the spindle were replaced in the cradles and all was ready. Dr. Baker was to make the first cut the next day. They had already marked the place where, following a straight line, there were no indentations showing through to the outside. It was reasonable to expect that this area was a margin between columns, a blank space such as had been found in the leather scrolls.

Allegro watched Dr. Baker make the final preparations, test the strings, tighten a bolt, and adjust the hanging saw and magnifying glass. Another magnifying glass would be strapped around Dr. Baker's forehead before he began the cutting the next morning, and could be lowered over his eyes should he need it.

Allegro had expected Dr. Baker to be nervous; instead, he realized that Baker was itching to start. The younger man was, therefore, not too surprised to get a telephone call from Dr. Baker late that night. In a breathless voice Baker confessed that he had not been able to wait for the morning and had already made the first cut. It was a success. The copper had not shattered. A strip had been neatly carved off and waited, undamaged, for Allegro.

In the morning the men examined it together. Nothing could be read; it was thick with cave dust. Fortunately, this dust fell away easily. What particles stuck in the indented words were removed by the gentle application of a small brush at the end of a dentist's drill, borrowed from the university's dental college.

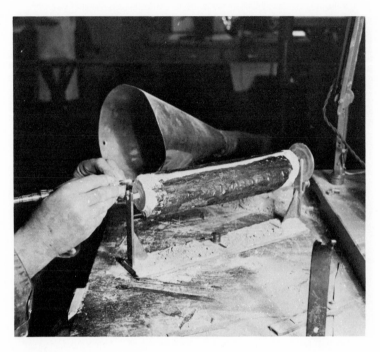

Removal of the scroll from the spindle

While Dr. Baker removed the scroll from the spindle to give it another coat of plastic and another baking, Allegro began translating.

The first words he read were: "In the Second Enclosure, in the underground passage that looks east, buried at eight and a half cubits, twenty-four talents."

"In the underground passes of the Holes, in the passage looking south, buried in the plaster at sixteen cubits, twenty-two talents."

"In the 'funnel,' silver from the consecrated offerings."

Dusting a section of the copper scroll

"In the pipes of waters that run to the basin of the drain, buried seven cubits from the wide part toward their mouth, nine talents."

John Allegro could not believe what he was reading. "Talents" and "silver" meant monetary treasure, buried treasure. Had Professor Kuhn been right, after all? Was this an inventory of buried silver and gold?

He made no report to Jerusalem until Dr. Baker had cut several more strips. It was not always possible to find the empty space of a margin, but by using the saw like a delicate jeweler's instrument, Dr. Baker was able in most cases to avoid cutting through words. Where it could not be avoided, the cut was made across a letter diagonally. When the strips were fitted together afterward, the whole letter was formed. A cut made vertically might have completely obliterated some letters.

Again Allegro cleaned and brushed each strip until he could read it. The scribe had used a sharp stylus to incise each letter into the metal. At the top of each column the words were large, but at the bottom they became cramped and less legible.

But when he had deciphered all the strips he communicated his belief to Jerusalem that the first half of the scroll, at least, contained a list of places in Jordan and Palestine where quantities of sacred treasure, vessels, gold and silver were buried. Of course, few of the places mentioned in the scroll still bear the same names today, and many of the references to hills, valleys and buildings were obscure.

Harding was encountering difficulties, and it was not until the end of 1955 that he could get official permission for the second half of the scroll to leave Jordan. During the period of waiting Allegro speculated on the scroll's secret inventory. Did it perhaps refer to the lost treasure of King Solomon's temple? Legends had persisted down the ages of the vast fortune hidden when the Temple was destroyed in the sixth century B.C.

Allegro thought it more likely that it inventoried treasure taken from the Temple during the Second Jewish Revolt in A.D. 132–135, perhaps by the Zealot leaders of

The copper scroll, finally cut apart and opened

the rebellion, who wanted to keep the sacred vessels and gold and silver from falling into Roman hands.

The second half of the scroll arrived in Manchester on January 2, and the final cuttings were made and Allegro's transcription of its contents was completed. The full scroll inventoried a wealth beyond that of an Aladdin. Translating the ancient measure of weight into modern terms, and even discounting for some exaggeration, the gold and silver listed in the scroll amounted to at least a million dollars in value.

Allegro believed the treasure had really existed and that at least some of it still lay buried, and undiscovered. But when the copper scroll and his transcription reached Jerusalem in April, 1956, de Vaux and the other scholars took a more skeptical view. They suspended comment until Milik's official study could be made and discussed with the scholars of the three sponsoring organizations. When this was done it was found Milik's reading of the scroll differed in some points from Allegro's.

Milik's version was also an inventory of treasure, but the conclusions drawn from it by de Vaux and others were not the same as Allegro's. They considered the possibility of a real treasure buried in Jordan and Palestine as extremely unlikely. And de Vaux stated that: "In the opinion of the scholars directly connected with the discovery, the list is not a real list of treasure, but is a collection of folk-lore stories about an imaginary treasure."

Several years later Allegro got financial backing and the approval of the Kingdom of Jordan and began a hunt for the treasure. The copper scroll became headline news, particularly in England, where he had found his backers. But, to date, not one single item of gold, silver, or, even a sacred vessel has been found.

In 1956 Harding and de Vaux had more than the copper scroll to concern them. Excavations at Qumran were nearing an end; the work of the Scrollery was continuing; and the Bedouins, in January of that year, had discovered still another cave—Cave Eleven.

Cave Eleven produced a rich haul—a long piece of a scroll of Leviticus, an Aramaic translation of part of the Book of Job, and many fragments from original Essenic writings. The most wonderful find was an almost complete scroll, the first since Cave One, with the exception of the copper scroll. It was a scroll of Psalms.

The need for securing funds to buy the Cave Eleven material occupied much of Harding's time. The financial drain was a constant one, since the Bedouins or Kando continued to produce, from time to time, fragments from the other caves as well. In fact, they had sold one small jar in 1953 which had been found in Cave One in 1947. De Vaux guessed that they had used it as a water storage vessel in the interim. This small jar was the only one found intact, except for the two purchased by Dr. Sukenik for the Hebrew University.

Kando had brought one mass of Cave Eleven fragments to Harding, who had admitted he had no money on hand to buy them. Kando was not disturbed and insisted on leaving them, saying: "You'll pay me. I trust you."

He would be paid but, in addition to money for these

The scroll of Psalms as it looked when found

The entrance to Cave Eleven: Located between Caves One and Three, it was the richest discovery after that of Cave Four.

purchases, more funds were needed for the Scrollery work. The money paid by McGill University and the other institutions had all been spent, but the translations were still unfinished.

Fortunately, all the team members were able to secure individual financing by institutions in their own countries, or from a Rockefeller educational fund. They no longer worked as a team, but were to finish their specific assignments at their own pace, coming to Jerusalem whenever necessary and when other duties permitted. This greatly reduced Harding's financial burden.

By now enough of the Qumran Old Testament books

had been photographed, studied and published so that some important conclusions could be drawn. In the sensation of the first discoveries newspapers had trumpeted the possibility that the Old Testament might be substantially changed. Jewish, Catholic and Protestant clergymen, too, wondered if the Qumran Biblical books would prove to be the oldest connecting link with the first authors of the Old Testament, and if there would be decided differences in the texts between the Qumran scrolls and current Bibles.

As it turned out, this was not so. What differences there were were rare, and were more a matter of wording than of the basic ideas of any book of the Old Testament.

The Qumran Isaiah scroll showed a definite affinity to the Masoretic text, with only slight changes of wording, and this was also true of the earlier fragments of Biblical works studied in the Scrollery. Scholars began to think this showed evidence of a direct line from the Masoretic Bible back to Qumran and from there to even older times.

But, in 1953, one member of the Scrollery team, Dr. Frank Cross, was cleaning pieces of the book of Samuel and reading as he went along, when he suddenly noticed that one passage differed distinctly from the Masoretic text. He brushed another fragment and read it; it contained a whole paragraph that was not in the Masoretic version of Samuel.

Fascinated, he went to the Scrollery library and checked the Septuagint text. It was word for word the writing on the Qumran scroll. By the time he had assembled all his pieces he could say definitely that this

198|

Qumran Samuel was in the Septuagint tradition, and not the Masoretic.

After that, more fragments of Biblical books turned up which were closer to the Septuagint wordings, or mixed Septuagint and Masoretic texts, as well as other variations.

It would seem that at the time of the Essenes there were prevalent several versions of Bible books, and that they had felt free to pick and choose from among them the wordings they preferred. This discovery left modern Biblical scholars the same freedom, since no one wording seemed more authentic than another.

The non-Biblical scrolls and fragments were a constant source of interest to the researchers—as they will continue to be to future generations of scholars. They threw new light on a very important period and place in history: Palestine of the first century A.D., and the centuries immediately preceding it. They contributed a body of new writings to Jewish literature, and new information about an obscure sect. The Essenes, unlike the Pharisees and Sadducees, are not even mentioned in the New Testament.

The heated controversies around the scrolls and their contents died down. A few scholars continued to doubt their age and authenticity, but the great majority accepted them. Although a few contended that Jesus and/or John the Baptist had been Essenes, the majority saw only little similarity and many differences between the Essene and Christian beliefs. The identities of the Teacher of Righteousness and the Wicked Priest have remained in doubt. Perhaps some future discovery will reveal more about them and tell us who they actually were.

CHAPTER XI

In 1956 HARDING RESIGNED his position as Director of the Jordanian Department of Antiquities, and moved to Lebanon. He and de Vaux had completed their excavations at Qumran, and the plateau showed a very changed appearance since they had first stood there, in 1949, and considered whether or not the small ruin was worth the trouble of digging up.

Now a large complement of rooms and courtyards lay exposed. Only the roofs were lacking to make Qumran appear much as it had two thousand years before. From the vantage point of the two-storied watchtower located in the northwest corner of the central, rectangular section that was the heart of the main building, it was possible to see the whole plan of the complex.

In the main rectangle were the council hall, the scriptorium where the scrolls had been written, the kitchen, pantry storerooms, and the central courtyard.

Only one other very important room was not part of this rectangle but led off from it southward. This room had probably been the dining and assembly hall, with a water cistern and a pantry on either side of it.

Spreading westward from the main building and its courtyard was a sprawling annex of four courtyards, four cisterns, the aqueduct entrance and settling basin, and numerous storerooms. Another, smaller annex adjoined the central building to the southeast, and here were the pottery kiln and pottery workshops, another cistern and settling basin and bath.

Many of the objects found in the excavations are now in the Palestine Museum for safekeeping against theft or destructive weather: the writing tables, plaster benches, inkwells, a quantity of reconstructed jars and urns and vases, lamps, pottery dishes and bowls, the jugs of coins. Other homely, everyday objects, however, such as the ovens, and pottery kilns and a basalt mill once used for grinding corn are still on Qumran.

Qumran itself has retained an air of expectancy. It is as if at any moment the mill will once again begin to grind, the ovens be heated and fresh loaves be baked, wet clay be slapped and turned to make the jars for firing in the kiln. No scholar who visits Qumran, or the few tourists who venture there, can fail to conjure up in imagination the sight of white-robed figures and the quick sound of sandaled feet moving through the rooms.

So much is now known about the Essenes that it is easy to visualize what they might have been doing in their typical daily rounds.

A scale model of the Qumran monastery constructed to plans published by de Vaux:

1. Outlet of the aqueduct into a large settling basin
2. Probable baptistry
3. The monastery's main gateway
4. The room in which the three juglets of silver coins were discovered buried beneath the floor
5. The tower
6. The communal kitchens
7. Steps rising to a wooden balustrade connecting with the tower
8. Council chambers
9. Scriptorium
10. Main water conduit
11. Workshops
12. Cattle shed
13. Hall of the congregation
14. Bath house (?)
15. Potter's workshop, with two kilns
16. Pantry of the refectory
17. Cisterns
18. Potter's mixing trough

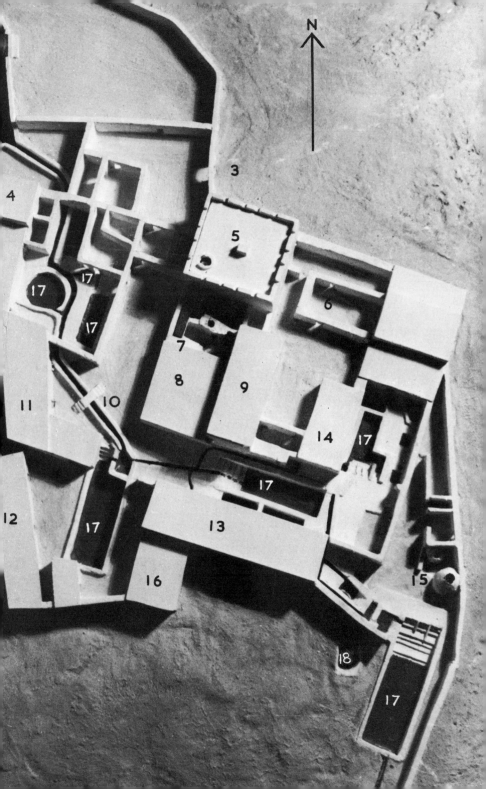

With the rising of the sun they would have come out of their sleeping tents and joined in the morning prayer. After the prayer they would wash and eat and then disperse to their many tasks, rigidly assigned, but subject to review and change each year. Some would go to Ain Feshka to work in the groves and orchards, or to get palm fronds to repair roofing. Some would tend flocks, others work in the tannery yard, in the kitchens, at the mill or the pottery kiln.

The rules forbade unseemly chatter while they worked, but work they did. Probationers were given three things: a white garment, working clothes—and a hatchet. This hatchet was probably not quite like its modern counterpart. It seems to have been an implement with many uses, and especially practical for digging.

One of its main jobs would have been to keep the water conduits cleared and open. Men must have been constantly employed in remaking the waterways, repairing channels and cisterns, cleaning sand and mud from the settling basin and outside aqueduct. As we know, the Essenes placed personal cleanliness high on their list of virtues.

The collection of fuel must have been a considerable problem, since both the plain and mountains are treeless. If they relied upon thorn bushes, dried grasses and whatever dead tree limbs they could get from around Ain Feshka, it must have been an exacting daily chore to keep kitchen hearths, bake ovens and pottery kiln going.

In all these tasks, whether the men were cooks, bakers, pantry helpers, scribes, herdsmen, salt gatherers, tanners or food cultivators, the Law they lived by imposed added hardships. They must not laugh too boisterously, or speak thoughtlessly. Probationers and even the most recently admitted juniors to the inner community, still on trial, had to be careful never to touch a senior. If this happened, the senior must stop his work and purify himself before returning to it.

The trial period was long, but probably not too long for those who must learn the rules. Once they were admitted to the innermost circle, punishments came swift and hard for transgressors. Gentle, peaceful and loving as they were to each other, their anger was terrible against anyone who sinned so greatly that he had to be expelled from their midst.

Josephus wrote an account of these pitiful unfortunates. Cast out from the community, they literally had no place to go. Still bound by the oath they had sworn to, they could not go to Jericho or other villages where they would certainly touch unbelievers and thus become defiled. They could not eat with strangers. They could not even eat an animal they caught with their own hands, since it had not been blessed by an Essene priest.

They hung around the Qumran plateau, living on grasses, growing weaker and weaker under the eyes of their former comrades. Only when they were close to starvation would the community sometimes take pity on them, feeling their punishment had been enough to cleanse the sin, and take them back.

Possibly because of their simple diet and vigorous life, many of the Essenes were long-lived. Some of them reached a hundred years of age. Yet death would claim them, and their numbers had to be replenished. Josephus has written that, since few of the Essene community married, they adopted children and raised them in the settlement. Perhaps these children were orphans, perhaps children of relatives. Qumran did not rely entirely upon children, however, to fill their vacancies. It might seem odd that new applicants, grown men, came to them of their own accord when the Law and the strict rules of the community deprived them of most of the enjoyments of ordinary life. But come they did.

They came because the Essenes offered hope. For centuries the Jews had been under the conqueror's yoke, Greeks, Egyptians and Romans, or under their own hated kings. Corruption and cynicism had flourished under all these rulers. Men were sickened by it and came to the exiled sect at Qumran to seek cleansing, a moral purpose and find hope in a great, triumphant future.

The austerity of the land around them suited the austerity of their lives. But, to match the glory of what they expected their future lives to be when the Messiahs came, they had only to lift their eyes from the plateau to the mountain in back of them and be refreshed by the sight of its colors, the soft and glowing pinks and purples, the shafts of gold when the sun struck the gray rocks. And the chanting of hymns was the sweetest of music, to their ears.

They had warning of Vespasian's approach. They may have sent out scouts to report on the danger, but it would not have been necessary. Josephus recounts that the Jordan River was clogged with corpses from Jericho, floating slowly down into the Dead Sea. The community would have seen these dreadful sights, forewarning them of their own fate.

Josephus paid high tribute to their courage. He wrote:

"And as for death, if it will be for their glory, they esteem it better than living always; and indeed our war with the Romans gave abundant evidences what great souls they had in their trials, wherein, although they were tortured and distorted, burnt and torn to pieces, and went through all kinds of instruments of torment, that they might be forced either to blaspheme their legislator or to eat what was forbidden them, yet could they not be made to do either of them, no, nor once to flatter their tormentors, nor to shed a tear; but they smiled in their very pains, and laughed those to scorn who inflicted the torments upon them, and resigned up their souls with great alacrity, as expecting to receive them again."

The scrolls had been hidden because of one war, two thousand years ago. Their discovery in modern times came at another period of strife. Even after the truce was signed between Jordan and Israel, the conflict went on. The continuous, accelerating clashes along the borders made it clear that there would be another outbreak of hostilities.

When war came it struck like lightning. The Six-Day War in June of 1967, although of short duration, was intensely fierce. Israel emerged victorious. Her boundaries were extended on the east to the Jordan River and the Dead Sea and included all of Jerusalem and the area of Qumran.

During and just after the war there were widespread rumors about the scrolls. What had happened to them? Had they been destroyed? Many people believed they had been carried out of the Museum and trucked off into the interior of Jordan, to Amman.

The alarms were false. When Israel took possession of all Jerusalem it was found that nothing had been disturbed or taken away from the Palestine Museum. Only the copper scroll was in Amman, where it had been for years. With the exception of the copper scroll, all the known contents of the eleven caves, plus those of the cave at Wady Murabba'at were now in the possession of the State of Israel. Some were at the Hebrew Museum, some in the Palestine Museum.

After Harding's resignation from the Department of Antiquities, the Kingdom of Jordan had repudiated his agreement with such institutions as McGill University, the Vatican and others, who were to have received scroll fragments for helping finance the Scrollery team. None of the allotted fragments had left the Museum.

During the Six-Day War Professor Yadin was concerned not only for the safety of the Museum's treasures but for *another* scroll which had been secretly in Kando's possession for seven years. How Kando had kept this hidden from Harding and de Vaux, how the information about it had leaked over the border to Yadin, are questions still not answered.

Perhaps, through devious channels, Kando had sought for a buyer in Israel. He wanted a million dollars for that scroll, which was a price the Jordanian Department of

Antiquities could not have paid. For whatever reason and by whatever means, the fact was that Yadin had heard of the scroll.

He had once been an Israeli general. Now, in 1967, on the day the Six-Day War ended, he organized a daring expedition. He took a special commando force of Israeli soldiers to Bethlehem, where snipers' bullets were still flying, and surprised Kando. The scroll was found and Yadin took possession of it for the State of Israel.

The details of the raid are not known. Yadin has stated: "I cannot at this stage disclose the way this scroll came into our hands, lest I endanger the chance of acquiring further scrolls." Some scholars deplore Yadin's raid. They feel that his aggressive action may have destroyed the trust between Bedouins and government officials and created the very danger which his statement wished to avoid.

Be that as it may, wherever the scroll was found (probably buried) the place had been unsuitable for its preservation. Since its removal from the dry cave it had sadly deteriorated, and some parts of it were now in very poor condition.

Nevertheless, it was a tremendous find. It was the longest complete scroll known, a meter longer than the Isaiah scroll. It must have come from a Qumran cave, since a description in it of a festival of the New Oil was the same as in another scroll part, transcribed by Father Milik. It also used the same Essenic calendar as did the other Qumran scrolls.

The new scroll included a set of religious rules; a

listing of sacrifices and offerings to be made at holy festivals; a hypothetical account of how an army should defend a king of Israel; and instructions for the building of a Temple.

Professor Yadin named it the "Temple Scroll," since the section dealing with the building of a Temple seemed to be the most important part of the text. It purported to be a commandment on how the Temple was to be built, and included the measurements for courts, side chambers, roofs and porch, and even set forth that it should have twelve gates named for the twelve tribes of Israel.

The Qumran plateau and the excavated settlement have been placed under the authority of the Israeli Department of Parks. When true peace finally comes to that troubled area, Qumran could become a magnet not only for scientists and scholars but a place of fascinating interest to travelers from all over the world.

The treasures of the caves are now part of the cultural wealth of Israel, but in a larger sense they belong to all of us. The scrolls enrich the religious and historical heritage of Christians and Jews, but to the Moslem Bedouins goes the credit for their discovery. And men of many different nationalities gathered in Jerusalem for the work on the scrolls, or studied them from abroad.

The story of the scrolls is a mosaic, made up of the large and small contributions of scientists and scholars, of a hundred different educational, religious, philanthropic or national institutions, and of ordinary men called upon, unexpectedly, to play their role in this drama of "the greatest manuscript discovery of modern times."

INDEX

Date Due